The 9
Mental Traps of
Corporate India

Dr. Prasad Sundararajan,
Geniuschoice Institute

&

Dr. V Mukunda Das,
Chandragupt Institute of Management Patna

The 9 Mental Traps of Corporate India

Dr. Prasad Sundararajan
Genius Temple, Geniuschoice Institute,
Kalimangalam, Alandurai, Coimbatore, INDIA

Dr. V Mukunda Das
Chandragupt Institute of Management Patna
Mithapur Institutional Area, Patna, BIHAR 800 001 INIDA

Printed at Kala Mudran, Patna
Phone: 9334330883
email: nipunnarain@gmail.com

Contents

The 9 Mental Traps
of Corporate India

Blessings from the Core Guide
Dr. Pradip N Khandwalla

"I specially welcome the book by Dr. Prasad Sundararajan and
Dr. V. Mukunda Das on mental traps or blocks. I am delighted
of course, that they have used an instrument which I developed
in the 1980s to study mental blocks for their pernicious effects
on creativity. Rarely have I seen an Indian study with such a
large sample as this book. The data shed light on what restrains
creativity and innovation in those Indians that are in decision
making positions or soon will be.

Expectedly, but also unfortunately, government officers seem to
have the highest mental blockage. This is unfortunate because
many of these government officials are vital agents for delivering
development and a variety of public services. Their being fearful
and risk averse bodes ill for initiative-taking and innovation.
I commend the book for raising the 'mindberg' for wider
scrutiny and also for explaining what needs to be done
to reduce mental blocks and traps.

My blessings for the success of the book and its impact."

...
TITLE NOTES

1

This book is a brief report on the creative-analytical study of the
mental blocks or mental traps [also called 'Psychological Traps']
of a special sample of 5,050 educated individuals of three categories
of employment or work settings.

- The Officers of Government Administration
- Managers in public, private, small scale sectors
- B-School students – considered potential managers

The data were collected during 1-2-3 days of seminars and-or training
workshops on the themes of 'mind-set analysis', 'ethics', 'genius leadership',
'creative-analytic thinking', and 'creative management'.

2

A 'Statistically validated and standardized' questionnaire developed
by Dr. Pradip N Khandwalla has been used for the data collection.
Though the larger sample included a population of 18,405 respondents
only the data from 5,050 are included in the main Tables. That sample
of 5,050 comprises those referred to in point 1 above. However, certain
special aspects of the larger sample of 13,365 respondents are mentioned
in relevant parts of the book to highlight certain observations.

3

The term 'you' printed anywhere in this book refers to the ones who
asked doubts and participated in the discussions or training workshops.
Moreover, most of the ideas in the book are taken from the recordings
from the Training-Analysis Workshops. The term 'corporate' means:
'of or shared by all the members of a group'.

What Else?

The intent of the book is to invite your attention to the truth of the phenomena of 'mental traps' and the way they affect the expressions, responses, behaviours, actions, and dialogues; work and relationships.

The mind is a directly sensed reality. But it is compared to an 'iceberg'. We use the term 'mindberg' in this book. Everyone must be sensing it, but only the tips. Almost every choice, decision, and action is primarily determined and guided by the deeper non-conscious realms of the mindberg. The presence of mind in the human entity is obvious especially in its aesthetic sensitivities about music, dance, art, poetry, natural phenomena, etc. It comes into clear manifestation during conflicting emotions or disturbing thoughts or experiences.

The supreme philosophies are all about the Mind.
Entire Psychology is about the Mind. Perhaps,
the entire human existence is about the mind,
by the mind, and for the mind.

The mind is filled with mind-sets. The mental traps are certain mind-sets located at the non-conscious realms of the mindberg, as they have been induced mostly during the development times. The mental traps prevent, restrict, and block the optimum development and evolution or the possible-probable 'entelechy' of the human entity. And what is a human entity? The most powerful entity on the planet Earth. Every rose is a rose is a rose and every cat is a cat is a cat – no nincompoop cats. The Vedic classics declare the originality and genius of the human entity: 'ayam-atma-brahma'. The western mystics stated: 'man is made in the form of the God'. The Rishis and Zen Masters declare that the possibility of enlightenment and Satori is present every moment or in every movement of the human entity. Then, what is the block?

Then what else is blocking the 'cat-ness' of the human entities other than the 'mental traps'? The potential of 'poornam' in the human entity is never opened to the doing of 'poornam-udachyate'. Only because of mental traps. The Sanskrit equivalent of 'genius' is 'nisarga', that means 'swa-bhava-nirmoksha': to do 'nir-moksha' or 'set-free' the 'bhavas' or potentialities of the 'swa' or the human centre. Yes, the doing is essential for the 'nir-moksha' from the 'mental traps'. From what else? IF considered genuinely, or if individuals are inspired for evolution and completeness of self and life and to achieve the happiness purpose of existence, the findings have the potential of triggering enlightenment about the mind-intellect-spirit and its creative powers. Knowledge about mental traps can invoke magical perceptions and perspectives about managing life, work, and relationships – at individual, group, societal, and national planes. The findings of the study carry unambiguous clues to drive radical, original, and great shifts in the destiny of Corporate India. Perhaps, of the very India.

The findings reveal that an incredible majority of educated-employed individuals carry 'medium' to 'high' mental traps. Individuals carrying 'medium -to- high' mental traps are a definite block to achieve the entelechies probable-possible for families, groups, associations, institutions, organizations, and nations. What else?

This book is a ground-breaking work from the vantage point of 'what else' implied in the previous paragraphs. The ideas, clues, and strategies carried in it can change the destiny of the very India. We carry no mental blocks or traps of doubt about it.

Sincerely.

Dr. Prasad Sundararajan & Dr. V Mukunda Das
15 August 2018

Please Note:

This book is set like a documentary film.

Certain critical ideas are repeated intentionally.

The parts are 'set' as a series of 'shots' about the details of mental traps.

Different shots may finally linkage into a perception of the whole story.

The subheads given in bold types comprised the PPTs whenever participants wanted a review of the contents of the workshops. When you finish reading the book, you may try making your own PPT about those ideas.

This book is extremely simple.

First of all, this book is just about 9 key ideas.

Its 'language and meanings' can be comprehended by Class X students. But, the reality of whatever denoted by that language is a 'doing' required on the part of your intellect and will.

Second of all, it reports no complex statistics.

Just the Mean percentage and Standard Deviation of the extent of mind-sets. But, that statistics is taken as a clear indicator of the tips-of-the-iceberg of the reality of Corporate India.

Third of all, only the simple peripheral aspects of the mind-sets are briefly explained in the book. If the mind-sets are within a limit then they are called 'mental blocks' and beyond it, 'mental traps'. Even with a peripheral grasp of those ideas, any reasonably sensitive individual can easily differentiate linkages of mental 'traps' in oneself and in others, as well as in the events and episodes during growth and development, schooling, workplace culture, media, campaigns, and so on. Even in the expressions, actions, and dialogues of Nations. You will recognise that the very human life is a tale of sound and fury signifying nothing but 'mental traps'.

Read the book with 'shraddha'.

Reflect as you read. And read, as you reflect.

Then this book will certainly do the magic in you.

The 9
Mental Traps of
Corporate India

Creative Analysis of 23+ years of data on 'mind-sets' collected by direct interface with 5,050 individuals comprising Senior Managers, Management Students, and Government Officers.

The mind-set percentages of the select sample of 5,050 are presented against those of a larger sample of 13,365 respondents of various other categories.

Here is a never-before and likely a never-again kind of data on the incidence of mind-sets that work at the level of mental traps in India. Do your own analysis, interpretations, and conclusions.

WHAT are the 9 'mental traps'?

1. Fear-Tension-Anxiety of Uncertain, Unknown, etc
Fears, tensions, and anxieties about the ambiguous, uncertain, complex, dangerous, strange, unknown, new, unexpected, etc; anxiety about the future, etc.

2. Centricity-Conformity
Obsession or compulsion to 'go with the crowd', allegiance to powerful forces, ideologies, etc; duplicated identity, conflict of identity. The 'majority mind-set'; 'statistical self', identity conflict etc.

3. Fear-Tension-Anxiety of Failure, Loss, etc
Fears, tensions, and anxieties about failure, error, defeat, weaknesses, being 'nobody'; non-acceptance, being sidelined, alienated, ostracized, etc.

4. Fear-Tension-Anxiety of 'Low-ness', Humiliation, etc
Fears, tensions, and anxieties about criticism, evaluation, humiliation, comparison, etc; obsessed about sense of 'low-ness'; inferiority feeling or inferiority complex.

5. Self-Doubt and Resource Myopia
Perceived or real incapacities and lack of confidence-in-self.

6. Functional Fixedness and Rigidity
Rigidity in thought, cognition, perception, dialoguing, etc; low analytic-powers; mechanical in expressions, responses, behaviours, actions, dialogues, work, and relationships.

7. Lack of Creative Sensitivity or Sensitivity-Lag
Low or lack of sensitivity to the higher order dimensions-aspects-attributes of life, self, work, nature, others, events, entities, things, and phenomena; poor intellectual grounding, poor reading and ideation;

poor quality social-network, idling, disused, intellect engines of reflection, imagination, visualization, intellectual-starvation during childhood, etc.

These seven mental traps are identified by the PNK-Questionnaire.

The remaining two mind-sets of traps have been differentiated out of observations and creative interviews with hundreds of trainees and others as well as observation and creative analysis of events, incidents, and media reports and articles on events and episodes of life, work, relationships.

The two other mind-settings of 'trapping nature' are:

'Familiarity-Contempt | Taken-for-granted Attitude Trap', 'Self-Importance | Speed Trap'.

NOTES
1
There can be several other 'individual-specific' mental traps also apart from the 9 referred-to here.
2
Mental traps 6 and 7 are linkaged to the 'intellect' engines [such as thinking, perception, conceptualization, reflection, imagination, visualization, intuition, projection, etc]. The first four and last two of the 9 mind-sets carry primary linkages with the 'emotive or emotional' engines of the mind, especially of fear, anxiety, and displeasure.
3
The term 'etc' is used plenty in this book. Because there are several linkages other than the ones mentioned to every concept, idea, event, thing, phenomenon referred to in the context of mindberg.

NOTES APPLICABLE TO THE TABLES

1.
The mean scores or average of the 'mind-sets' are given
for the Corporate sample of 5,050 respondents along with
those of another larger sample [N: 13,365] are presented
for comparative analysis.

2.
The concept of 'Sub-sample' refers to the category of
sample indicated in the titles of the respective tables.

3.
The 'Larger Sample' consisted of 13,365 respondents who
belonged to categories other than those of the 'Corporate'
sub-samples, such as: the students of plus 2, university courses,
professional courses, diploma and certificate programs,
housewives, job-applicants, visitors at Genius Temple
and trainees of Geniuschoice Institute, etc.

The space provided below every table may be used to jot
down your observations and analysis such as comparing and
contrasting the average scores of different combinations of
sub-samples, vis-a-vis the larger sample, the sample with
low or threshold mental-blocks, and so on.

The Extent or Percentage of the First 7 Mind-sets of Corporate India

The mind-set percentages of the first 7 mind-sets are assessed by the PNK-Questionnaire. They are reported in the seven Tables given in the subsequent pages - as listed below:

Table 1: The average mind-sets of Public Sector Managers

Table 2: Average mind-sets of Private Sector Managers

Table 3: Average mind-sets of IT Professionals,
Junior, Senior, and Top-Management Levels

Table 4: Average mind-sets of B-School Students

Table 5: The average scores of mind-sets of IAS-IPS-IFS
Probationers at LBSNAA, data collected: circa 1991

Table 6: Average scores of mind-sets of
Government Officers and Administrators

Table 7: Percentage of mind-sets scores of 87 respondents
with average scores below 20 per cent
[Threshold mental 'blocks' or 'essential level of
mental-blocks']

Note:

There are 7 more tables placed at relevant locations in the book. They are about the larger sample of 13,365 respondents.

LEGEND:

1. Mind-set Scores BELOW 19% indicate 'Threshold Blocks'

The 'Threshold Mental Blocks' are mind-sets that are considered essential requirements for survival and sustenance, adjustment + adaptation with signals, things, people, events, entities, and phenomena of existence.

Mind-set Scores 19% and ABOVE indicate Mental 'TRAPS'

2. Mind-set Scores of range: 19% - 36%
'LOW' Mental 'traps' – Low disadvantage

3. Mind-set Scores of range: 37% - 54%
'MEDIUM' Mental 'traps' – Medium disadvantage

4. Mind-set Scores of range: 55% - 75%
'HIGH' Mental 'traps' – High disadvantage

5. Mind-set Scores beyond 75% indicate
'SEVERE' mental traps

About the Data [N: 5,050 + 13,365]:

The findings are based on 'participatory* and directly collected data' from 5,050 [managers, administrators, management students] and 13,365 respondents of other categories [university students, school-college teachers, job applicants, visitors in education exhibitions, etc].

*Participatory data - in the sense that every questionnaire was directly administered to 'participants' of training workshops of durations of 3 or 2 or one day, on 'genius leadership', 'creative-analytic thinking', 'mind-set analysis', and seminars on related themes.

The data from a lager sample of 13,365 respondents were collected in the usual ways of Questionnaire administration.

The Statistically validated questionnaire of 40 items is referred to in this thesis as 'PNK-Questionnaire' [developed by Dr. Pradip N Khandwalla, Ex-Director of IIMA, and a globally renowned researcher in Creativity]. Like any 'standardized' questionnaire, it provides the finest approximation of responses.

As the questionnaires were administered under 'controlled environments' of rigorous training workshops and sessions, the critical points were explained and doubts clarified in greater details. The very base of the programs and workshops comprised analysis of the questionnaire data and creative-feedback about the results. Therefore, the authenticity of data could be ensured in all probable-possible completeness of the extent to which a questionnaire can be used for data collection.

Table 1
Average scores of the mind-sets of
PUBLIC SECTOR MANAGERS [N: 704]

| Sl. No. | MIND-SETS | Average percentage of mind-set scores | |
		Sub-Sample** N: 704	Larger*** Sample
1	Fear and Anxiety of Ambiguity, etc.	45%	51%
2	Centricity and Conformity	38%	42%
3	Fear and Anxiety of Failure, etc.	39%	44%
4	Fear and Anxiety of Low-ness, etc.	30%	36%
5	Resource Myopia and Self-Doubt	27%	32%
6	Rigidity and Functional Fixity	39%	46%
7	Sensitivity Lag	38%	44%

***Larger Sample [N: 13,365]: The larger sample population at the time of the reported statistics – include respondents other than administrators, managers, and management students.

Table 2
Average scores of the mind-sets of
PRIVATE SECTOR MANAGERS
[N: 951]

Sl. No.	MIND-SETS	Average percentage of mind-set scores	
		Sub-Sample** N: 951	Larger*** Sample
1	Fear and Anxiety of Ambiguity, etc.	43%	51%
2	Centricity and Conformity	35%	42%
3	Fear and Anxiety of Failure, etc.	37%	44%
4	Fear and Anxiety of Low-ness, etc.	29%	36%
5	Resource Myopia and Self-Doubt	26%	32%
6	Rigidity and Functional Fixity	38%	46%
7	Sensitivity Lag	36%	44%

***Larger Sample [N: 13,365]: The larger sample population at the time of the reported statistics – include respondents other than administrators, managers, and management students.

Table 3
Average scores of the mind-sets of IT Professionals
JUNIOR, SENIOR, AND TOP-MANAGEMENT LEVELS
[N: 1,207]

Sl. No.	MIND-SETS	Average percentage of mind-set scores	
		Sub-Sample** N: 1,207	Larger*** Sample
1	Fear and Anxiety of Ambiguity, etc.	48%	51%
2	Centricity and Conformity	38%	42%
3	Fear and Anxiety of Failure, etc.	45%	44%
4	Fear and Anxiety of Low-ness, etc.	37%	36%
5	Resource Myopia and Self-Doubt	30%	32%
6	Rigidity and Functional Fixity	43%	46%
7	Sensitivity Lag	43%	44%

***Larger Sample [N: 13,365]: The larger sample population at the time of the reported statistics – include respondents other than administrators, managers, and management students.

Table 4
Average scores of the mind-sets of
B-SCHOOL STUDENTS [N: 1554]

Sl. No.	MIND-SETS	Average percentage of mind-set scores	
		Sub-Sample** N: 1,554	Larger*** Sample
1	Fear and Anxiety of Ambiguity, etc.	51%	51%
2	Centricity and Conformity	38%	42%
3	Fear and Anxiety of Failure, etc.	46%	44%
4	Fear and Anxiety of Low-ness, etc.	38%	36%
5	Resource Myopia and Self-Doubt	32%	32%
6	Rigidity and Functional Fixity	48%	46%
7	Sensitivity-Lag	46%	44%

***Larger Sample [N: 13,365]: The larger sample population at the time of the reported statistics – include respondents other than administrators, managers, and management students.

Table 5
Average scores of the mind-sets of IAS-IPS-IFS
Probationers at LBSNAA, data collected: circa 1991 [N: 73]

Sl. No.	MIND-SETS	Average percentage of mind-set scores	
		Sub-Sample N: 73	Larger*** Sample
1	Fear and Anxiety of Ambiguity, etc.	38%	51%
2	Centricity and Conformity	32%	42%
3	Fear and Anxiety of Failure, etc.	33%	44%
4	Fear and Anxiety of Low-ness, etc.	27%	36%
5	Resource Myopia and Self-Doubt	25%	32%
6	Rigidity and Functional Fixity	34%	46%
7	Sensitivity Lag	33%	44%

***Larger Sample [N: 13,365]: The larger sample population at the time of the reported statistics – include respondents other than administrators, managers, and management students.

Table 6

Average scores of the mind-sets of GOVERNMENT OFFICERS [N: 561]

Sl. No.	MIND-SETS	Average percentage of mind-set scores	
		Sub-Sample** N: 561	Larger*** Sample
1	Fear and Anxiety of Ambiguity, etc.	59%	51%
2	Centricity and Conformity	73%	42%
3	Fear and Anxiety of Failure, etc.	73%	44%
4	Fear and Anxiety of Low-ness, etc.	46%	36%
5	Resource Myopia and Self-Doubt	53%	32%
6	Rigidity and Functional Fixity	59%	46%
7	Sensitivity-Lag	59%	44%

** The sub-sample [of N 561] does not include the IPS-IAS-IFS samples referred to in Table-5.

***Larger Sample [N: 13,365]: The larger sample population at the time of the reported statistics – include respondents other than administrators, managers, and management students.

Table 7
Average mind-sets** of respondents
with general pattern of scores indicating only
'Threshold Mental Blocks' [The <u>Essential</u> Mental 'Blocks']
N: 87 [within the sample of 5,050 respondents]

Sl. No.	MIND-SETS	<u>Average percentage of mind-set scores</u>	
		<u>Sub-Sample**</u> N: 87	<u>Larger***</u> <u>Sample</u>
1	Fear and Anxiety of Ambiguity, etc.	23%	51%
2	Centricity and Conformity	6.6%	42%
3	Fear and Anxiety of Failure, etc.	13.2%	44%
4	Fear and Anxiety of Low-ness, etc.	13.2%	36%
5	Resource Myopia and Self-Doubt	6.6%	32%
6	Rigidity and Functional Fixity	19.8%	46%
7	Sensitivity Lag	26.4%	44%

** The scores are significantly low and below 19% cut-off point [except #1], therefore, considered 'essential mental blocks', instead of mental 'traps'.

***Larger Sample [N: 13,365]: The larger sample population at the time of the reported statistics – include respondents other than administrators, managers, and management students.

What is a mental trap or mental-block?

To begin with, what is the so-called 'mind'?

**To the context, here is a definition of Mind:
'Mind is nothing but Mind-sets'**

Normal day-to-day life activities, work or job and role functions, survival-sustenance activities are managed by appropriate and relevant mind-sets. All knowledge or 'knowing', knowledge about 'doing' and 'being' are mind-sets. All ideas and ideologies - whatsoever - are all but mind-sets. Whatever is known as creativity, originality, genius etc too are driven by relevant mind-sets. The original mind or the mind of a newborn is but 'empty' of any mind-sets. The Zen mystics used the idea, 'the mind of no-mind' to refer to a mind that is 'free' from any of the usual mind-sets of the majority - at least.

Key concept: Block
- An obstacle to the normal progress or functioning of something
- To stop something from happening or succeeding
- To be between two or more things preventing connection or interaction or potential linkages with higher order or quality and power of functions of something

These meanings are applicable in cases of mind-sets that would 'block' or stop a response, behaviour, or action from happening, or in biasing interaction with some people, situations, or settings in the environment outside or states inside. The blocks induce feelings and emotions of fear, anxiety, tension, etc.

What is a mind-set?
The term 'mind-set' may appear a bit technical, but some 'state of mind' is always sensed by every human being. Even little babies, birds, and cats can sense the signals of the state-of-mind of other animals as well as human beings.

Take a few minutes and observe events, people, settings, signals, things, and phenomena of human existence. In almost every item you will be able to discover linkages of your mind-sets about them. You will easily identify the complex interplay of mind-sets that generate perceptions [for example of good, okay, bad, great, etc] about those items.

When you say, 'I am an Indian' to someone else, 'Indian' refers to a mind-set also. For instance, in India, there is the Tamil mind-set, Kerala mind-set, Gujarati mind-set, and so on because of the social, historical, and cultural differences in learning-development history.

Values such as honesty, integrity, ethics; attitudes, needs, interests, etc are all but names that differentiate mind-sets of various types. There are mind-sets about one's own 'self', inner self or real self, body, mind, intelligence, intellect, spirit; social, religious, economic, familial, academic positioning; about job or work role; and about positions required for situations of life-survival-relationships, about purpose and meaning in life; linkaged with the hierarchy of drives, motives, and needs.

Mind-sets about the body, 'self-image' – such as male or female or hermaphrodite; mind-sets about the very mind itself; mind-sets about oneself as creative, original, talented, genius, innovative, etc. Mind-sets of self-image as a singer, dancer, artist etc or as useless, unethical, criminal, antisocial etc also. As a result of education and experience, mind-sets are developed vis-à-vis one's learning, training, and experience – such as student, teacher, father, mother, doctor, engineer, manager, leader, and so on. A human being cannot exist without mind-sets. At least a mind-set of 'no-mind'.

Mind-sets are induced, taught, trained, enforced etc during the so-called learning-development process. Most mind-sets are 'duplicated' or imitated from models in the environment, media, schooling, etc. For a few individuals, the mind-sets evolve into creative, original, genius, and enlightened by certain coincidences or incidental linkages. The entire growth and development of human beings involves formation of mind-sets. Of Knowing-Doing-Being. About expressions, responses, behaviours, actions, dialoguing, work, and relationships.

Language and Mind-sets

Once language is developed, countless individual-specific mind-sets are liable to be formed. By the great power of language, countless mind-sets are induced, formed, duplicated. For example, the mind-sets of religions, various ideologies, norms, conditions, regulations, classifications, divisions, separations, and so on some of which may facilitate formation of mental traps.

The language of ongoing stream of thoughts, dialogues, or from reading or media gets instantly linkaged to correlated mind-sets of immense range and variation. Language reinforces and expands most of the mental traps. Language also carries the great power to trigger and develop new, creative, and original mind-sets. [Therefore, the great advantage of good reading].

By regular interaction with people, significantly great number of mind-sets are induced, trained, enforced as well as duplicated and imitated. Such mind-sets tend to drive the responses, behaviors, actions, and dialogues; the level and quality of life, work, relationships - whatsoever be the learning and education, the role-positions, identities, and other possible-probable linkages of a person. There can be mind-sets about all kinds of 'names', and about 'knowings', 'doings', and 'states-of-being' such as:

- teacher, student, manager, leader, driver, carpenter, …etc
- father, mother, son, daughter, wife, husband, lover, …etc.
- master, guru, mentor, guide, mystic …etc.
- university degree holders, IAS, IPS, MBA, BTech, MBBS,…
- several types of rulers, clerics, traders …etc

The apparent identicality or similarity of a mind-set in two or more individuals may contain aspects that are totally different in the different orbits in the mindbergs. And, this reality of individual differences renders all the complexities of human behaviour, especially in the context of inter-personal relationships. This makes the process of managing and leading a complex phenomenon; whether of a small group or a large organization.

Thus, the role and functions of language-driven mind-sets:
- to drive the direction of sensing, cognition and perception, observation, attention, reflection, memory or thinking, analysis, conceptualization, and sensitivity;
- to linkage with mind-sets related to the item being sensed; projected, imagined, or cognized-perceived, etc;
- and thereby drive responses, behaviors, actions, and dialogues.

Mind-sets may exist and function at the conscious, sub-conscious, and unconscious orbits of the mindberg. However, the mind-sets that function as mental traps reside in the much larger unconscious orbits of the mindberg.

THE MINDBERG

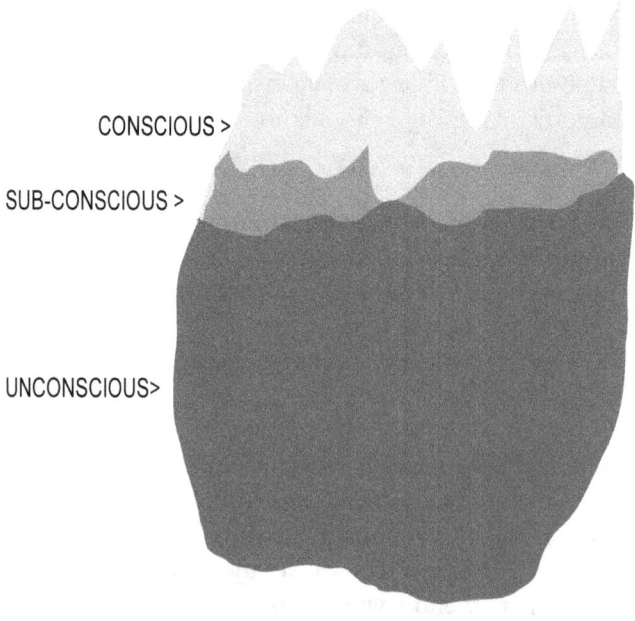

CONSCIOUS >

SUB-CONSCIOUS >

UNCONSCIOUS>

Mental 'blocks' and
Mental 'TRAPS': The DIFFERENCE

The intent of the 40 items in the PNK-Questionnaire is to assess certain mind-sets that resist, block, prevent, regulate, and control the responses, behaviors, actions, dialogues, work, and relationships of human beings born and brought up in the social-economic-cultural-educational milieu of India. [The PNK-Questionnaire is presented at the end of this book].

The items in the questionnaire have been differentiated on the basis of rigorous 'statistical procedures' such as Principal Component Analysis, Factor Analysis, Validity-Reliability tests, etc.

The PNK-Questionnaire scores are converted in to percentages.
The scores are categorized into 'Threshold Blocks'; followed by 'Low', 'Medium', 'High', and 'Severe' Traps based on 'concept validation' vis-à-vis the relevant literature in Psychology and Psychoanalysis as well as creative analysis of the probable-possible consequences of such mind-sets.

The mental 'TRAPS' are
functionally different from the mental 'blocks'

1
In reality, all the 9 mind-sets are essential or even inevitable for survival-sustenance and adaptation with the people, things, events, entities, phenomena, environment, and larger society. Such essential pattern of mind-sets are called 'threshold mental blocks'. **That 'essential-ness' is the reason why those mind-sets are induced purposefully as blocks into every child.**

In fact, no human being can escape from forming such mental 'blocks'. Because, forming of mental 'blocks' is a natural outcome during the early development and the inevitable learning process. Absolutely inevitable for the human species. Unlike the birds and cats. That's why such 'blocks' are inevitable chapters of the penal codes of every land.

29

Throughout history, human 'natural expressions' are 'blocked' whenever there are groups. All rules, regulations, behaviour codes, norms, mores, folkways, and so on are for 'blocking' the variations of behaviours of individuals and groups of all kinds.

2

All the mental 'blocks' may turn out to become mental 'traps' depending upon the extent and expanse of restriction and disuse of the engines of the mind and engines-of-intellect. Then the consequences are just the opposite. In other words, if a mind-set is more than the required ['threshold' level 'blocks'], then it actually converts itself to function like a trap preventing the very development and evolution of individuals. It is somewhat like the quantity of food required for a time and consuming extra to the point of diseases.

Imagine 'physical' blocks and traps – then you will get a sense of the way and design of the mental 'blocks' and mental 'traps'. Most of the mind-sets that are linkaged with mental 'traps' are formed during the non-conscious times. Therefore, they are powered by the emotive forces of anxiety-fear-displeasure; that too are located in the non-conscious realms of the 'mindberg'. In fact, the extent and pattern of mental traps are an indicator of the nature of learning-and-development history of individuals.

3

As one is always with his or her mindberg, or mind IS the very self ['person' is for the others, observers, etc], it's ways of functions cannot be discerned. But its manifestations such as fear, conflict, etc are sensed. Mental traps are mostly driven by mind-sets in the non-conscious realms of the mindberg. The non-conscious part is not directly-easily accessible for resolution or editing or resetting [unless implosive experiences or training in mind-set analysis]. Yet, they induce conscious responses, behaviors-actions, dialogues and relationships, create direction for social-networking, etc.

WHAT IS A MENTAL TRAP?

Key-Concept: Trap
- An enclosure or device, often baited, for catching animals, usually by affording a way in but not a way out.
- A trick betraying a person into speech or an act, response or behavior.
- An arrangement to catch an unsuspecting person.

The term trap is used with all the concept sense and connotations of the word meanings of the term. There is already the concept of 'psychological block'. But it implies relatively simple 'mental inability or inhibition caused by emotional factors'.

The margin between mental 'blocks' and mental 'traps'
Mental 'blocks' simply block any irrelevant, undesirable, unacceptable, disadvantageous expressions, responses, behaviours, dialogues, actions, and relationships. For instance, by fear-tension-anxiety of the unknown and ambiguous, strange or new, the person may just avoid such situations smoothly. Like the child was prevented and controlled by the parents. The purpose of inducing mental 'blocks' was to protect the child, to ensure safety and security, as well as to follow the established paths of success in survival-sustenance, to sustain happiness and equilibrium. However, the extent of induction often misinterprets and manipulates the reality actually faced by the developing child. Heavy doses of mental 'blocks' lead to conversion them into mental 'traps'.

The external environment of life-work-relationships would demand a range of expressions, responses, behaviours, dialogues, actions, and relationships quite different from what the child experienced at home. They may demand responses-behaviors-actions of much greater levels than taught and trained at home. As a result, the mental 'blocks' expand and evolve into mental 'traps'. The concept of mental-blocks or mental traps are relatively easy to comprehend. Yet, those 'names' refer to highly complex and equally subtle phenomena of the mindberg and intellect. There are different 'orbits' of linkages to every one of them.

31

1. Every mental block-trap consists of a network of several orbits of mind-sets that are formed during the early development times of the human being. Such mind-sets were induced, enforced, trained, and insisted with the purpose of actually 'blocking' the eccentric or random and undesirable responses, behaviours, actions, etc of the growing child.
2. The mental blocks-traps tend to drive or govern most of the expressions, responses, behaviours, dialogues, and actions, as well as work and relationships of human beings.
3. The mental-blocks-traps are resident in deep non-conscious mindberg. Because, the major load of mind-sets [that eventually become mental traps] are formed during the early development times [from birth to about 23 years]. This 'learning' [every mind-set a learning] may continue expansion of mind-sets into different orbits perhaps till the last minute of existence [depending upon various factors such as existent mental-blocks-traps, and events in the environment, etc]. For instance, there can be the sudden formation of a mind-set that the world is a perception, the very self an illusion, etc just before the last breath.

+++

A question: If human beings are shaped after the so-called Almighty God, if all roses and birds and cats are equally competent, then WHY the entelechy of the 'knowing', 'doing', and 'state-of-being' of human entities follow the normal distribution curve-?

Answer: Just due to mental 'traps' and mental 'traps' and mental 'traps' only. What else can block the entelechies of a human being..! Mental blocks-traps decide and drive the ways in which attitudes are manifested, opinions and views conveyed, responses-behaviors-actions-dialogues are expressed; the way a work is executed, and relationships managed.

The basic three differences between mental 'blocks' and mental 'traps':

1

The mind-sets of blocking nature are a definite requirement for survival-sustenance and adaptation with environment and society. Mental 'blocks' therefore, facilitate individual development and evolution. They are mind-sets of low powers. Just making the individual sensitive to the relevant aspects – that require control and adjustment of responses-behaviors-actions, etc. But mental 'traps' do not allow the person to make responses-behaviors-actions or develop competencies of work and relationships.

For instance, a threshold level of 'centricity and conformity' is absolutely essential for survival and sustenance, adaptation with the environment, people, procedures, systems, rules, regulations, and even within oneself. However, higher degrees of 'centricity-conformity' would drive the person to adopt severe restrictions to behaviours, actions, relationships, etc without any concern for independent will and decision making regardless of the demands and actual requirements. Bureaucratic mind-setting is one of the several consequences.

2

In case of a mental trap, the will or self of the person gets trapped like a rabbit or rat in a trap. A mental 'block' induces 'mild' tension or anxiety, fear, feelings of apprehension, hesitation, worry, etc. A mental trap induces 'medium to high to severe tension, anxiety, fear, etc. For instance, take the case of a person who is capable of singing, who sings alone at home or in small gathering of friends. He would hesitate and escape the scene if compelled to sing on a stage before a large audience. Yet, others can persuade him to the extent of making him sing at least on a subsequent occasion or even in the same location. He can be virtually pushed on to the stage and finally he would perform. He has only a 'block': mental-block. But, if his is a mental trap, then he may even fall down unconscious if he is pushed onto the stage.

In fact, the manifestations and evidences of mental-blocks-traps can be more or less easily differentiated by attention-to-details of the evidences of a reality faced, observation of the expressions, responses-behaviors-actions and work and relationships of people around.

3

In the case of mental 'blocks', the individual can bypass or escape the block whenever really required. The boy is aware that his fear of humiliation prevents him from trying for a music competition; or fear of failure affecting the performance in tests or examinations, or interviews. He may eventually overcome it. But, mental 'traps' would trigger-induce nervousness, severe tension, psychosomatic consequences, etc. Due to mental 'traps' significant number of students refrain from the very learning of text books. A 'good' candidate may fail in tests and interviews.

If not properly identified and resolved, those mind-sets operate like a rabbit-trap: more panicky the rabbit, the trap becomes more tight and complex. The very nature of its movements are conducive to tightening of the trap. However, one can transcend or bypass all the mental 'traps' by creative self analysis [reflection, attention-to-details, re-conceptualization of self-image, etc] and related strategies of 'doings'. Certain basic strategies for 'trap resolution' are proposed in this book.

PROBLEM: The very mental traps prevent awareness about them.
Some what like, one cannot discern one's own defects. Because, the ongoing mind functions within the boundaries of its existent mind-sets, and therefore, also of the mental-blocks and mental traps.

The 'Inverted 'U' Curve'

The 'inverted U' curve explains the relationship between mental 'blocks' and mental 'traps' vis-a-vis performance of some activity; the spontaneity and creativity of the self, life, work, relationships settings. The 'blocks' work as sort of gentle warning signals of mind-sets that make the individual aware of the situation and the need for good, correct, complete performance. But the 'traps' are oversupply of fear and anxiety and tension that will work just the opposite.

The threshold mental-blocks 'help and facilitate' adjustment and adaptation with the requirements of life, work, relationships; survival-sustenance activities; acceptable patterns of expressions, responses, behaviours, actions, work, relationships, and dialogues. As well as serving the motives of love, and belongingness, and self-esteem. In other words, the 'threshold-level' fear or anxiety or 'tension' is good or powerful a driver of complete and effective or creative performance. But extra dose of anxiety and tension may block or prevent even the very performance itself. School is a training centre for developing the feeling of tension and anxiety. A well-prepared session, interview, or presentation may go haywire just because of high anxiety-tension'; symbolised in the downward part of the inverted 'U' curve.

Food is essential but too much of it causes severe health hazards. Medicines are very useful. But too much of it or over dose can lead even to death. Sexuality is natural and beautiful, but beyond a point or uncontrolled expressions can invite physical or moral dangers. Life is wonderful but if someone living for a thousand years would want to die out of boredom.

The Universality of the 'Inverted-U' Curve

Please do not stop at the easy 'knowing' it.
Try translating that knowing into the doing of reality-testing.

SEE the LINKAGES** of the Inverted-U Curve everywhere:
IN the expressions, responses, behaviours, actions, and dialogues.
In the manifestations of all possible-probable mind-sets. In managing
the requirements of the body, mind, intelligence, intellect, and spirit.
In managing life, self, others, work, and relationships. In the attempts
to accessing enlightenment or Satori.

**Notes on Linkages and Linkage Perception
Almost 90 per cent of creativity involves 'Linkage Projection'.
The rest is in Linkage Discovery and Linkage Creation.
The entire world is nothing but linkages. All subject matters
are descriptions of linkages and their orbits and networks,
as the very language itself is.

In linkage creation, it is mostly practical, physical, and manifested
externally. The entire range of tools, devices, and equipment; systems,
processes, and procedures; engines, designs, structures; mobiles, and
laptops, and automobiles, and so on are linkage creations. Whereas all
fiction, poetry, art, music, dance, craft, drama, film, etc are based on
linkage projection. However, all these are functions involving three or
more of the engines-of-intellect. With the support of the freewheeling
mind + flow opened attendant-spirit [the will to do the 'doing' of such
creations].

However, it requires experience in driving the engines of intellect
with the support of the trap-free mind. The method of VIOLIN
[Variant-Invariant-Orbit-Linkage-Intentionality-Network Analysis]
is very effective in providing the required range of practice for the
engines of intellect. The method is presented in the book,
'The Missing Engines of Management Education',
Prasad Sundararajan, Amazon.com

Concluding points about mental 'Blocks' and mental 'Traps'

The 9 mind-sets, when operate as mental 'traps', block or delimit or prevent the original expressions of the powers of the engines of mind, intellect, and spirit. The mental 'traps' sort of betray the self of a person. For instance, a mental trap would induce great desire or aspiration, need or want or craving on one side and on the other side, prevent the required level and quality of work to achieve them. They induce bias in the expressions, responses, behaviors, and dialogues. They delimit the elegant, correct, completeness of work and relationships.
And many more individual-specific consequences.

The most critical aspect:
The mental traps blocks the genius inherent in every standard human entity.

- Mental 'blocks' or mental 'traps' are made up of indefinite number of smaller units of mind-sets. The 'blocks' are different from 'traps' mainly in the extent and expanse of anxiety, tension, fear, etc.
- All the mental 'blocks' are essential for survival-sustenance and social adaptation ['threshold blocks']. But mental 'traps' are dysfunctional and work as blocks to individual evolution to higher expressions and entelechies. In other words, mental 'blocks' beyond the threshold scale function as mental 'traps' – too much of anything is negative in state and consequences.
- All mental 'blocks' or 'traps' have linkages with emotive states or emotions and feelings.
- Mental 'blocks' or 'traps' are involved in most of the expressions, responses, behaviors, actions, dialogues, work, and relationships.
- No human being can exist without mental 'blocks'. Even 'sub-human creatures' may carry mental 'blocks' [and mental 'traps' of their level and functions if trained by human beings]. But every human being can escape from the mental 'traps'.

From the vantage-point of the linkages mentioned above, it may be stated that the very life of human beings is a game of mental 'blocks' and mental 'traps'.

Note:
Try to conceptualize your perceptions and insights about the
mental blocks and mental traps, their implications or consequences
in behaviours, actions, work, self, life, in managing relationships, etc.
Finding it a difficult or complex task itself is a sinal of mental blocks
or mental traps [depending upon the extent of difficulty sensed].
Try for more ideation after finishing the book.

The 7 Intelligence Traps
Adapted from 'Thinking Course', Edward De Bono, Pentacor BV, 1986

Finding of Edward De Bono - 1
A highly intelligent person can construct a rational and well-argued case for virtually any point of view. Especially those aspects which he or she has already learnt and understood.

TRAP 7
The more coherent this support for a particular idea, the less the thinker sees any need to accurately explore the situation and look for alternatives. Eventually, his or her degree of confidence becomes increasingly dependent upon that intelligence [or knowledge] and therefore, tends to avoid 'ambiguous' ideas, events, situations, experiences, etc. The 'any' point of view may include even the dysfunctional and rigid aspects that block the learning-development of the person - as well as of others.

Finding of Edward De Bono - 2
The ego, self-image, and peer-status of a highly intelligent person are often based on that intelligence.

TRAP 6
From this arises the need to always be right, correct, clever, conventional, bureaucratic, and norm-bound. Block: From this the inherent tendency of 'openness' is closed.

Finding of Edward De Bono - 3
Verbal fluency is often mistaken, in school and after, for thinking competency and communication competency. As a result, the person learns to sustain his or her self-image, self-esteem, and self-concept on the basis of this verbal ability.

TRAP 5
The sheer physical quickness of verbal fluency tempts the person to jump to conclusions from a few signals.

Finding of Edward De Bono – 4
The critical use of intelligence is always more immediately satisfying than the creative and constructive use. To prove someone else wrong gives instant achievement of superiority and sense of 'self-importance'.

TRAP 4: 'Self-Importance'
This also leads to a judgmental and evaluative mode of perception, cognition, and thinking by which the creative and original processes are put into disuse.

Finding of Edward De Bono - 5
Highly intelligent minds often seem to prefer the certainty of 'reactive' thinking [solving puzzles, sorting data, categorizing, classifying, etc]

TRAP 3
This leads to the tendency to prefer to clear information, instruction, established ideas, majority supported beliefs, values, perspectives, etc. Reactive thinking [that is, thinking about things from a pre-existent knowledge-base] restrains projective or creative thinking [where the thinker has to create the setting of ideas, etc].

Finding of Edward De Bono – 6
High intelligence, comprising factors mentioned above [logic about the available 'knowings', verbal fluency, reactive thinking-dialoguing, high academic grades, etc] confuse quick understanding with thinking competency or creative thinking and 'slowness' with being 'dull-witted'.

TRAP 2
This preference for quick comprehension tempts people to reject anything new [as anything new would take some time for reflection and incubation]. In history, almost every new idea, a new thing, or a unique or creative person was rejected, defeated, or even destroyed first.

The 'doings' of a <u>creative mind-setting tend to be 'slower'</u>
[especially in interpersonal settings], because:
[1] it takes some time for 'reflection' and 'incubation',
[2] it has to take in more data, and
[3] it has to look at the thing from different vantage points in order
to derive multiple perceptions - before reaching a final conclusion.
Taking time to perceive the totality of a problem or a new situation
is an important first step for creative thinking.

Finding of Edward De Bono - 7
**The highly intelligent person is frequently encouraged [by the benefit-
oriented, short-term advantage oriented, technique-driven mediocrity
or majority] to place a higher value on cleverness than on wisdom
[correct perception, thinking, and cognition derived from reflection
and incubation employing the creative and original processes upon
direct observation or experience of a reality or situation].**

TRAP 1
Reinforced by the support and apparent appreciation of the 'others'
['centricity-conformity'], the highly intelligent mind-settings tend to
become arrogant and aggressive. Individuals of 'highly intelligent' mind-
settings develop an inability to appreciate the specializations, differences,
contributions, and uniqueness the others can bring to organisational
entelechy.

+++
Edward DeBono, claimed and declared in his book titled 'The Happiness
Purpose' that, it requires creativity or freedom from mental traps in
order to create and-or discover true happiness in life. To discern the
true purpose of one's only one existence. It cannot be achieved by great
'intelligence' or 'knowings' alone. Including 'knowings' about how to
develop happiness from the sermons and classics and self-help
texts and talks.

A cat-level human being must be seeing the invisible, hear the unspoken, and identify the unique strengths of oneself as well as other people around – definitely for his or her development as well as to perform the role-functions as a creative manager or genius leader - the requirement of the present and future. Only a creative individual is a creative individual is a creative individual. One cannot be creative in the morning and non-creative in the evening. And, only a creative individual can ever be a creative manager. The creativity required for the role functions of a manager shall not be mistaken as the creativity in poetry, painting, dance, theatre, physics, engineering, etc.

And, certainly, the number-one requirement for creativity or originality or genius is the freedom from mental traps. From what else? What else can block the wonderful engines of the marvellous human entity?

NOTE
Do a self-analysis about the extent to which you are blocked by the 'Intelligence Traps'. IF.

The Mental traps:
The First Orbit* of Expressions

If the trinity of 'knowing', 'doing', and 'being' are considered the basic components of the human entity; the mental traps are the most blocking to the 'doing'.

Almost all the mental traps block or prevent the quality and completeness of 'doing' and the scope to evolve to the 'higher states-of-being'. The very purpose of existence is in 'doing'. The universe exists in its 'doing'. The very body too. And, certainly, it will be one of the super-most 'doings' - if it is directed towards differentiating the mental traps.

The 9 mental traps are not precisely water-tight compartments - nothing inside the mindberg is in such state, though. There can be same 'consequences' for different mental traps. Yet, each one of the nine mental traps carry its own linkages and effects on the responses, behaviours, actions, work, relationships, and dialogues of an individual.

The mind-sets of mental traps-blocks are defined and described in simple words and sentences that are easy to grasp. But the simple words indicate only the tips-of-the-iceberg of the 'realities' referred-to by them. For instance, the concept of 'fear-tension-anxiety' is very familiar but the 'reality' of that emotive states experienced by the mind could range from a mild and rudimentary feeling of tense expectancy about something to serious obsessive-compulsive states by which a person might end up in madness or commit suicide or fratricide.

However, the brief descriptions can provide sufficient clues to reflect upon and develop approximate clarity of 'knowing' and 'doing' about the 9 mental-blocks [or mental traps when the blocks are of medium to high strength].

*First Orbit of Expressions or Manifestations of Mental Traps:
Most of the 'first orbit' of description about mental traps are adopted
from the book, 'The Fourth Eye' of Pradip N Khandwalla. The remaining
two orbits are identified by creative-analytic interviews, observations
of thousands of respondents and trainees, events and episodes in the
environment reported in the media, popular fiction and films, and
from the literature of Psychology.

Mental Trap 1
Fear-tension-anxiety of Ambiguity, Uncertainly, Complexity, New, Strange, Unexpected, etc.
'Obsession with Comfort-Zones', 'Routines', 'known ways', 'clarity', etc

Key word: Ambiguity:
- Vagueness, obscurity, confusion
- Open to more than one interpretation
- Having a double meaning
- Unclear or inexact because a choice between alternatives has not been made

This mental trap drives the emotions of anxiety, panic, fear, tension,
feeling of apprehension, etc about aspects that are ambiguous or
uncertain, unknown, strange, new, expected, etc. Feeling irritation,
hesitation, diffidence, disturbance, worry, conflict, doubt, hatred, anger,
etc about the ambiguous, uncertain, new, etc; entailing an inability to
manage vague situations and experiences, negative conditions or
illnesses of body, worrying-depressing thoughts, etc.

NOTES:
1. The 'aspect of ambiguity' can be in an idea, concept, event, person,
thing, entity, or phenomenon - in the external environment or in the
internal environment. Increasingly it is going to be the VUCAD world:
Volatile, Uncertain, Complex, Ambiguous, and Dangerous world.
2. It need not be always any clear feeling of anxiety or fear or tension.
But often manifested as a typical lack of tolerance for the strange,
unexpected, new, unfamiliar, ambiguous, unclear, etc.

3. This Mental Trap of fear-tension-anxiety of ambiguity-uncertainty drives responses, behaviors, actions, dialogues; work and relationships in ways:

- of sustaining or creating 'comfort zones' ...
- resorting to duplicated or imitated responses, behaviors, actions, and dialogues ...
- an aversion to unknown, unclear, unfamiliar, unexpected, and strange things and phenomena ...
- the attitude of opposition or repugnance ...
- any habitual dislike, antipathy, unwillingness about the new and unknown ...
- avoiding new situations, challenging, ambiguous, strange, or unfamiliar situations ...

- 'compulsive activities': everything to be structured or organized ...
- to get tense, offended, irritated, defensive, defeated, disappointed, frustrated, etc with unexpected situations, contexts ...
- giving more importance to quick-grasp of the peripherals rather than understanding through reflection and insight ...
- viewing an ambiguous situation | task insurmountable or avoidable rather than a challenge or a new learning experience ...

- resort to 'ego defense mechanisms' [Sigmund Freud] or 'ego advance mechanisms'***
- tend to develop 'depression', 'sense of meaninglessness', 'ennui', 'loss of value or purpose in life or work or relationships, etc. *** [Ego-defense mechanisms listed elsewhere in the book].

Note:
Certain ideas and ideologies can sometimes become powerful to induce-invoke-trigger tension, or anxiety, or fear in individuals and gradually expand to whole populations. The Indian media do not seem to differentiate that aspect. AS a result the negative and 'sensational' news are given heavy prominence.

Mental Trap 2
Centricity and Conformity

Centricity-Conformity at trap levels [especially 'medium to high'] denotes unverified or blind allegiance to powerful forces, ideologies, etc despite inner disagreement. It implies 'duplicated identity or conflict of identity'.

In conformity-trap, there is the element of compulsion-obsession about following the attitudes, norms, beliefs, opinions, views, ideologies, etc of the majority, powerful-others, group or social network. **Despite actual evidences of realities that contradict the required conformities.** Individuals with high conformity-trap would often hold blind adherence to certain beliefs and notions without bothering to question their validity or usefulness in today's world or to the 'reality' of one's own life, work, and relationships.

Centricity refers to the tendency to adopt or duplicate or imitate the expressions or behaviours, actions, dialogues, etc of the majority, powerful others, so-called celebrities, rich and famous individuals, social network, etc. **Centricity is in externally manifested** responses, behaviors, and actions. **Centricity is mostly in the ways of actions, behaviour, 'doing' something, and in relating to people.**

Centricity-trap is driven by a 'compulsion' to imitate or duplicate the majority [social network] ways of responses, behaviors, actions, and dialogues. The intent is mostly to appease the others, or to protect the status and role in relevant groups, etc. It is driven by the compulsion to belong to the relevant groups regardless of true attitudes, values, opinions, etc. This trap is an exaggeration of the requirement to adapt and adjust with the ways of the group.

This mental trap of 'centricity-conformity' is sustained by the fear of 'ostracization' or fear of 'alienation' or due to tensions about the possible-probable expressions of one's own 'eccentricity' or free will.

The core difference between conformity and centricity is that, the former resides in the internal world and the latter is in the behaviors and responses to the external world. However, they may operate in contradiction also. For instance, a person may really trust and believe in something, an idea or value or norm. Yet, he or she may behave just the opposite of that - due to the force of centricity. A divorced spouse may want to go back to old relationship yet centricity-trap of the person or the group or family prevents it. A common example is the unethical behaviors such as bribery, nepotism, etc despite clear awareness and belief in truth, honesty, integrity, etc.

From the vantage-point of this centricity-trap, it is possible-probable that a good number of people resort to corruption by the centricity of accumulating riches and monies, possessions and popularity. People end up buying things to sustain their centricity with a reference group. Regardless of economic grounding.

Typical expressions of the mental trap of 'centricity-conformity':

- bureaucratic mind-setting ...
- conventional attitudes, needs, interests, preferences ...
- fear of 'powerful others', feeling tension to face them ...
- obsessive concern for what is expected or regarded as normal...
- customary behavior, appearance, etc ...
- tension and fear of social disapproval - obsessed with socially acceptable behavior; ail to appreciate and reward new ideas, expressions, etc of others and-or of oneself ...
- strong allegiance to customs, rituals, traditions, folkways, etc...
- Tendency to duplicate safe and guaranteed procedures and practices, etc without reflection [about its precise relevance] ...
- preference for risk-free existence ...
- t'to-be-in-the-good-books of others' syndrome ...
- fear of 'loneliness'; fear of darkness, of illnesses, fear or tension about ideas of death, etc ...
- tendency to manic reactions, 'hysteria' behaviours, and actions ...
- .

- conversion of psychological stress and tension into physical symptoms ['somatization'] or a change in self-awareness [such as a fugue state or 'selective amnesia'] ...
- 'Paradoxical Compulsion' to respond-behave-TALK-act like the 'others': centricity [paradoxical, because everyone is supremely convinced about their uniqueness. But what comprises their uniqueness is severely unclear] ...
- to believe, accept, agree with the majority, rituals, norms, etc: conformity [internal or ideological]; tendency to be 'other-directed' [other-directed: in Psychology - of person|s or their behaviour, governed by external circumstances and the behaviour and standards of 'others'] ...

Mental Trap 3
Fear-tension-anxiety of Failure, Challenges, Future, Loss, etc

The concept of 'failure' is indicative of all possible-probable situations that resemble failure-like experience or perception. Situations of error, fear about 'error-in-retrospect' ['wrong dots getting connected some time later'], defeat, loss-deficiency; weakness of any kind, non-acceptance, being 'nobody'; being sidelined, alienated, and ostracized, etc carry linkages with this mental trap.

Typical expressions driven by this mental trap:
- risk avoidance ... avoidance of probable-possible failure in responses, behaviors, dialogues, and actions and life-work-relationships ...
- failure perceived as 'loss of esteem or image' ...
- obsessed with 'comfort zone' ...
- confused about the responses, behaviors, and actions never tried before [trapped in the familiar and known] ...
- avoiding situations or events where a performance is likely to be evaluated or compared to others - especially if such situations or events are of a competitive nature - primarily because the individual feels incapable of handling them ...

- viewing failure at any task as a complete loss of face with the accompanying fear of being labelled as a useless person ...
- extreme difficulty, tension, in taking decisions ...
- lacking the courage, or feeling tense, especially in a competitive environment or settings ...
- anxiety, panic, or tension when faced with situations of defeat, challenges ...

Note:
Fear-tension-anxiety of failure has linkages with anticipatory avoidance of future miseries. Fear-and-anxiety about the future is based on certain memories of the past of self, or stories of misery and defeat of others ['anticipatory anxiety'].

Mental Trap 4
Fear-tension-anxiety of humiliation and 'low-ness', inferiority feelings, anxiety of 'comparison' and criticism, etc.

- anxiety and fear about humiliation-embarrassment, feeling perpetual, ongoing, or anticipatory 'low-ness' ...
- 'touchiness' [shame, indignity, ignominy, disgrace, discomfiture, dishonor, degradation, discredit, belittlement, etc especially by 'comparisons', etc] ...
- fears-and-anxieties about comparison, ridicule, side-lining, alienation, criticism, evaluation, opposition, etc ...
- fear-and-anxiety of being 'nobody'; fear-and-anxiety of non-acceptance, error, defeat, being ostracized, etc - linkaged to fear-and-anxiety of loss
- 'Inspiration-Suppression' ...
- conflicting self-image ['What the others would think about me, if I do or talk out or behave a certain unique way..!']...

The ego-advance mechanisms may convert this mental traps into expressions, responses, behaviors, actions, and dialogues connoting envy, anger, hatred, enmity, antagonism, aggression, and such strong emotions and feelings.

Feeling insulted and intimidated and offended for comments and critiques. This mental trap of anxiety about low-ness and inferiority is likely to have effects of:

- fear or anxiety or tension about expressing uniqueness ...
- suppressing even strong inspirations or needs and wants for fear of criticisms or oppositions ...
- 'duplicated self-image' [or pretending more than what the individual is aware of about himself or herself] ...
- This mental trap determines the type or level of 'social network' and inter-personal relationships ...
- anxiety-fear-apprehension about 'others' or some impending calamity
- pre-empting criticism, negative labelling, humiliating responses, behaviors, and actions, expressions, from others ...
- fear of 'being different'; 'tender self' ...
- frail self-esteem or lack of ego strength ...
- difficulty in team 'adjustment' and 'relationship management' [not necessarily team 'work'] ...
- lack of emotional competencies ...
- interactions strictly restricted to familiar, non-tense, comfortable, like-minded people, etc.
- unrealistic self-appraisal and the negative aspects of oneself or close associates and relatives are overlooked for fear of 'self-humiliation' or feeling inferior ...
- closed even to constructive criticism due to 'comparing' ...
- blocked to training and development interventions ...

By the mental trap of fear, tension, and anxiety of 'low-ness', one feels 'good' before low population or individuals and groups. And feel 'low' or bad when interface with 'high' populations and 'powerful or famous individuals.' In other words, you 'feel' good-right-correct emotions before low populations and 'bad' emotive states before high populations.
But a rose does not feel low before the Banyan tree.
A cat does not feel low before a huge human being.

By this mental trap the comparison process works in a dysfunctional way for the already blocked or weak mind-sets and feel threatened when confronted with high settings. The Adlerian theory of personality is about the feeling 'low' or inferiority feelings and inferiority complex. Mostly, even desire for self-actualization and self-realization could be driven by the low-high mental traps than by genuine sensitivity to the attendant-spirit inside or force outside.

People refrain from admitting even simple mistakes they committed because, the people around will start looking down upon them. Even those who have confidence may not accept their mistakes, because of the fear-and-anxiety of humiliation. Most settings of humiliation and low-ness is based on direct or indirect 'comparisons'. This is a comedy of the genius-loci of India. The land of 'Aham Brahmasmi' and 'Vasudhaiva Kudumbakam'.

Mental Trap 5
Resource Myopia and Self-Doubt

Self-Doubt: Missing engines of 'self-trust'
Note: Try to grasp the probable-possible manifestations of 'resource-myopia' by reflecting upon the very meanings of the keywords:

Resource-resourceful:
- one's personal attributes and capabilities regarded as able to help or sustain one in adverse circumstances
- the ability to find quick and clever ways to overcome difficulties
- initiative, ingenuity, talent, ability, capability

Myopia:
- nearsightedness
- lack of imagination, foresight, or intellectual insight

Self:
- The operating entity within the individual, whatever is referred-to by the words 'I', 'me', 'my', etc.

Concept sense of Doubt:
- a feeling of uncertainty or lack of conviction
- unsureness, indecision, hesitation, suspicion, confusion
- apprehension; hesitancy, vacillation, irresolution
- scepticism, distrust, mistrust, cynicism, uneasiness

This Mental Trap denotes the following:
- 'Identity Conflict' – clarity versus vagueness of self ...
- doubtful about one's potentialities ...
- lack of 'Self-Trust' ...
- 'Self-doubt' whether one can be really competent in higher planes of 'knowing' or 'doing' or achieving a 'state-of-being' ...

NOTE:
All of the preceding four mental 'traps' are linkaged primarily with the emotive states-of-being of 'fear, tension, and anxiety'. Therefore, they are 'emotional blocks' unlike the subsequent two mind-sets, which are 'intellect blocks-traps'. The term 'intellect' refers to the engines of observation, attention, perception, cognition, reflection, conceptualization, intuition, projection, imagination, etc.

Mental Trap 6
Rigidity and Functional Fixedness [an Intellect-Trap]

Rigidity is the opposite of 'flexibility'.
Flexibility in thinking and reasoning is well known as a critical engine in 'creative' ideation and activities.

Functional Fixedness refers to the relative inability to apply 'variations' or changes - despite requirements or availability of models and guidance - in the way an activity is performed. The activity can be of learning or 'knowing', 'doing', or the way a mind-set is sustained or the attachment with certain 'state-of-being'.

Typical expressions of the trap:

- lack of flexibility in observation, dialoguing, thinking, response patterns, actions, behaviors, etc.
- rigid linear thinking - 'parrot thinking'
- strictness, severity, harshness in thoughts-ideas, attitudes, etc ...
- trapped in the past, in the past glories, happiness in identification with well known and powerful others, etc ...
- 'Newtonian Mechanical' world-view, self-view' others-view ...
- strong dependence on 'thoughts' than 'direct experiences' ...
- strict in opinion, observance, procedure, or method; admitting or allowing no deviation; scrupulously exact or precise, unchanging, unvarying; not adaptable in outlook or response...

- blind adherence to certain beliefs and notions without bothering to question their consequences or evidences
- believing that everything or every individual has a specific function within which he or she has to function - with no room for change ...
- looking at life or work by a formula approach, or a single vantage-point, resisting any changes in approach ...
- uncomfortable with new ideas and new ways of responses, behaviors, and actions, tension from one's own thoughts ...
- rigidity in 'Self-image'
- rigidity in attitude, approaches to people, perceptions, analysis etc - taken as consistency, mastery over mind, etc ...
- rigidity in attitudes, perspectives, ideologies ...
- getting violent or irritated when ways of 'doing' are questioned ...
- biased processes of the engines-of-intellect, especially thinking, conceptualization, dialoguing, message processing, etc ...
- analysis based on duplicated or unverified logics ...
- replication of imitated ready-made analyses ...
- 'Functional-fixedness' in the ways of engine-of-intellect [attention, reflection, perception, conceptualization, etc] ...
- lack of flexibility: in observation, attention, thinking, response patterns, actions, behaviors, ways of dialoguing, internal-dialogue, etc ...

- low tolerance for errors and mistakes and faults, 'bads', wrongs, incorrect, etc of 'others' and-or of oneself ...
- poor quality of 'Analytic-Thinking'; no variation allowed ...
- 'Functional-Fixedness of the very mental traps' ...

Mental Trap 7
Sensitivity-Lag and Signal Myopia
Lack of Creative Sensitivity [an Intellect-Trap]

Sensitivity-Lag here refers-to the 'missing' mind-sets and engines of:
- sensitiveness to the hidden, invisible, intangible, and subtle aspects or linkages of entities, things, phenomena in Nature; within self, others, etc
- originality, reactivity, responsiveness
- finer feelings and understanding, empathy, intuition
- receptiveness; perceptive, creatively analytical
- thoughtfulness, tact, diplomacy, delicacy, subtlety, finer feelings; understanding, empathy, sensibility, feeling, intuition, discernment, insight.

By sensitivity-lag, there is the lack of attention-to-details, lack of any future perspective despite goals, purposes, aims, etc. The self becomes trapped in the peripheral, ordinary, easy-to-notice kind of evidences. The higher order details of existence remain unnoticed, uninspiring, etc. The evolution of the self is trapped in primitive states-of-being.

Genius, creativity, originality, discovery, etc require sensitivity to expressions, responses, behaviours, dialogues, and actions of people; signals, things, events, entities, and phenomena. Creative sensitivity is essential to 'hear the unspoken, to see the invisible, to draw the unique strengths of people, and much more - to look at reality from different vantage points'. A good lot of problems and conflicts of all kinds, wars and struggles, and so on are only due to the lack of creative sensitivity. Of individuals, groups, organizations, or nations.

Disused Engines of Sensitivities: Missing Creative-Sensitivity Consequences:

- poor attention-to-details resulting in the disuse of original sensitivities of the entity to signals, cues, clues of all kinds especially, the more critical linkages of the 'invisible-hidden-subtle orbits' of
referred-to-reality [in the context and-or requirements] ...
- poor observation, reflection, and conceptualization ...
- nothing is 'created' out of sensing entities, phenomena, uniqueness, etc. in the external world; no new perceptions created about oneself too despite unique experiences ...

Sensitivity-Lag and the concept of 'Signal Myopia'
[Signal Myopia: Poor 'signal detection' capacity]

All kinds of 'signals' or cues and clues are available in the environment outside [and inside]; only the known and familiar and 'conformed ones' are sensed or detected. All kinds of thoughts or intuitions and insights are possible for the original engines of the human entity. Yet, only the trained and reinforced ones are noticed and reflected upon. The parents-teachers-guides block or prevent the 'original search responses' of the child.
Their mental traps make them 'myopic about the signals of greatness' concealed in the expressions of the child.

Typical expressions of sensitivity-lag and signal myopia:

- poor observation, low power attention, lack of attention-to-details, poor reflection, conceptualization, imagination, etc ...
- intellectually starved development background ...
- no reading or poor or easy and casual reading choices ...
- poor quality, mediocre peer group and schooling experiences ...
- no hobbies, interests, talents, etc [due to lack of creative sensitivity to one's own intuitions, feelings, sensibilities ...
- lack of 'sensitivity' to the 'deeper' aspects of events, entities, things and phenomena ...
- low quality idea generation, dialogues, writings ...

- tendency to manifest violent, insulting, intimidating, injuring ways of language [words-sentences] regardless of education, role position, maturity, etc ...
- tendency towards lazy-diffident behaviors and responses ...
- peripheral sensing of data or idea from reading, discussions, etc ..
- lack spontaneity; tend to be 'pretentious' ...
- poor interest in the arts, poetry, Nature, mysteries, aesthetic aspects, etc.
- fail to fantasize, lack 'rich' experiences of life, etc ...
- suppress expression of tender or genuine emotions ...
- exert pressure on self and others to keep emotions under control and to be rational ...
- low or zero tolerance for errors and mistakes and faults, wrongs, incorrect, etc of 'others' ...

Out of all, sensitivity-lag is a crucially disadvantageous mental trap because it blocks the fundamental nature of the organism, every cell of the organism. The entire nature-process works by sensitivity - reciprocal sensitivity. The plants, insects, birds, and cats survive by sensitivity. The sub-human creatures survive by direct sensing of signals such as of temperature, light, chemicals, electricity, magnetic field, etc. The great Vedas and other treatises about the universe etc had been created and developed by the ancient rishis and mystics by the power of their sensitivities. Nevertheless, the primary sensitivity engines are highly active in every human being. Evidence: they possess items of art and craft, enjoy dance and music, film and other entertainments and aesthetics around. Seldom attempt to do the 'doings' of them, though.
Just due to mental traps.

Creative Sensitivity is the foundation of Genius.

"Asking what genius is, is like hiding loot in one's pocket and declaring oneself innocent."
[Adapted from the book: Zen Flesh, Zen Bones,
by Paul Reps and Nyogen Sensaki, Shambhala Pocket Classics, 1994, Page 210]

Creative-Sensitivity is the greatest engine of intellect. The most remarkable difference of the human entities vis-a-vis all other species. See a genius-level definition of leadership as follows:

"... the essential qualities of leadership and the acts that define a leader: the ability to hear what is left unspoken, humility, commitment, the value of looking at reality from many vantage points, the ability to create an organization that draws out the unique strengths of every member."

[W. Chan Kim and Renee A. Mauborgne, Parables of Leadership, Harvard Business Review, July-August, 1992, page 123]

+++
Quote:
Tech billionaire parenting
"Viewpoint" [by Alice Thomson in the Times, March 14, 2018]

"Melinda Gate's children don't have smart phones and only use a computer in the kitchen. Her husband Bill spends hours in his office reading books while everyone else is refreshing their home page. The most sought-after private school in Silicon Valley, the Waldorf School of Peninsula, bans electronic devices for the under-11s and teaches children of eBay, Apple, Uber, and Google staff to make go-karts, knit and cook. Mark Zuckerberg wants his daughters to read Dr Seuss and play outside rather than use Messenger Kids. Steve Jobs strictly limited his children's use of technology a home. It is astonishing if you think about it: the more money that you make out of the tech industry, the more you appear to shield your family from its effects".

The Forming of Mental Blocks and Traps: 'Inevitable'

The world, the environment of survival and sustenance is such that forming of mental blocks-traps are inevitable.

Managing blocks, bypassing blocks, transcending blocks is the quintessential of the very existence of all things, entities of all species, and phenomena.

See the pervasive presence of 'blocks' in the very design-setting-process of the world and in the human entities.

For instance:

- Blocks at the physical level: food, clothing, and shelter. They are not available free and easy. The food items are much less in proportion to the requirement of every species.
- Blocks at the social level: norms, customs, regulations, etiquettes, folkways, traditions, etc.
- Blocks at the individual personal level: present in all learning and development activities. Tests and examinations to progress from one level to the other in schooling.
- Blocks at the body level. The majority of populations do not learn and develop any special abilities and competencies.
- Blocks at the intelligence level: some learners are 'blocked' in grasping certain subjects such as Algebra, Chemistry, Philosophy, etc in which some others are easily excellent.
- Blocks at the engines-of-intellect level: incompetent in thinking, attention-to-details, perception and cognition, reflection, conceptualization, imagination and visualization, etc. Every child manifests evidences of creativity, originality, and genius. But the environment blocks them.
- Blocks at the will or attendant-spirit level.
- **Finally, the trained-induced-enforced blocks of the mind-settings of** fear-tension-anxiety of humiliation-failure-uncertainty, centricity-conformity, resource-myopia, etc.

THE ESSENTIALITY OF MENTAL 'BLOCKS'
[NOT of mental 'TRAPS']

Why minimum or threshold mental 'blocks' are essential-?
If the so-called mental 'blocks' are not induced-enforced-trained in a child, his or her expressions, responses, behaviours, actions become like a river without its banks or a kite without string-control. Mental 'blocks' are like strings that guide the kite to move around among other kites and according to the wind conditions. They are like gears for an automobile. They are like grammar in language. Like optimum required dress on the naked body.

Therefore, because of the sheer necessity of survival and sustenance, the developing mind-setting of the child must be imbued with certain 'blocks'. [To repeat: if the 'blocks' are beyond the threshold limits, then they become 'traps' that prevent the child from his or her possible-probable development and evolution, subsequent real-ization and actual-ization of entelechies].

Key Concept: Essential
- absolutely necessary; extremely important
- fundamental or central to the nature of something or someone
- a thing that is absolutely necessary
- the fundamental elements or characteristics of something
- in Biochemistry - required for normal growth but not synthesized in the body and therefore necessary in the diet.

So, the mental 'blocks' are extremely essential for managing self, life, and relationships. Essential for managing appropriateness and approximation of expressions, responses, behaviours, actions, work, dialogues, and relationships according to requirements, contexts, and in maintaining and sustaining comfort zones. [The comfort zones of safety and security of the mind, body, intelligence, intellect, and spirit. The mental blocks and mental traps ensure sustaining the 'pleasure principle'].

Primarily, the mental 'blocks' are essential because of the very nature of the engines of the mind itself.
The original powers of the engines-of-mind are vast and primitive. Its primary expressions are random and eccentric. The Freudian concept of 'Id' or stock of basic instincts – the primary state of mind at birth, implies animal instincts, blind motivation to seek 'pleasure' and 'need gratification', etc.

The 'Id' works by the 'pleasure-pain principle': to seek pleasure and to avoid 'pain'. Yet, despite the inner drive to avoid 'pain', the very mind is ever ready to drive the child to touch and pull anything and everything, goes to dirt and danger, search into every possible opening, food and filth in the same way. Only the human child would ingest its own excretions. The child begins by being driven by its 'original search response' other than the basic drives of hunger, thirst, security, and love [present in all beings by which their survival is rendered possible].

The ways and nature of the original mind, or mind at birth, is very dynamic, free-wheeling and eccentric. This incessant flow of eccentric expressions can be observed with almost any child of standard body and health. Therefore, the wild flow of the original mind is to be necessarily subjected to controls and restrictions, shaping and 'refining', by using negative strokes and even physical punishments to B-L-O-C-K whatever responses, behaviours, actions, relationships, and dialogues that are negative, dysfunctional, injurious, dangerous, disadvantageous, etc to the child as well as for the others.

The situations that induce mental blocks would appear very logical and valid. For instance, the uncertain, unknown, strange, new, etc may appear obviously threatening even for the one with below 'threshold levels' of fear-tension-anxiety. For instance, fear-and-anxiety or tension about the ambiguous prevents entry into uncertainties and thereby from needless confusion and conflict. Rigidities and functional fixities are maintained, sensitivity-lags sustained, etc for the same reason. The mental blocks provide or sustain an internal comfort zone and 'approximated' balance of the mind.

The teaching-training-guiding that induced the blocking mind-sets occurred mainly during the non-conscious developmental times. As the findings of this long term data show, almost everyone in the operating environment would carry mental traps who in turn may dissuade or prevent the responses, behaviours, actions, work, and dialogues of the block-free individual. They may abandon, ostracize, or annihilate the one with free-wheeling mind. If not, they would be sidelined by labelling 'eccentrics'. Perhaps, the parents or teachers, or media and milieu do not intent to induce 'trapping' level of mental blocks in the developing child. But the dynamics of life, work, relationships are such that the interactions end up inducing mental traps.Certainly, unintentionally.

THE LOGIC OF MENTAL 'BLOCKS'

**Why the mental-blocks are enforced in a child
will be clear if the logic involved is grasped clearly.**

The mind-sets in the design of the PNK-Questionnaire are considered at five levels by the score percentages: 'threshold mental-blocks' which are essential and beyond it are low, medium, high, and severe 'mental traps'.

From the beginning times of creativity research, the 'mental traps' have been identified as dysfunctional and disadvantageous for individual evolution and higher order performance in any field of activity.

The mind-sets of mental 'blocks-traps' may seem to be inter-linkaged to an extent, especially by the emotive forces of fear and anxiety and the feeling of 'anxiety, fear, and tension'. For instance, the mind-sets of fear and anxiety are common to the mental blocks of 'centricity-conformity', in dealing with failure, humiliation and comparison, ambiguity and uncertainty. Yet, the mind-sets of every mental block are different from one another. However, some of the mind-sets may belong to different blocks-traps.

There is a clear logic about why the parents-teachers-guides are obsessed about 'blocking' as well as 'shaping' the responses, behaviours, and actions of children or even adults. The logics are derived out of the following kind of 'realities':

1. The plenty of evidences of threats, challenges, barriers, dangers, uncertainties, strangenesses, newness, unexpectedness, etc in the environment - from which the child is to be protected.
2. They [parents-teachers-guides, etc] are of different range of attitudes, values, ethics, capabilities, etc. For example, this provides the logic for-of mental trap 1, namely fear and anxiety of ambiguity, uncertainty, strange, new, etc.

3. The 'statistics of society' as well as individuals and groups enforce, persuade, insist the requirements of compliance, obedience, commitment, etc to rules, regulations, code of conduct, ideologies, attitudes, etc. This provides the logic for the 'conformity' side of mental trap 2.

4. One has to behave, respond, act, talk, eat, move around, marry, live, etc according to the ways demonstrated-modelled-campaigned, etc. Maintaining the expressions and behaviours, etc is considered relevant to whatever mind-sets of identity of the developing child.

5. Individual has to express responses, behaviours, dialogues, and actions with people; answer to questions; officials can anytime monitor any individual, and so on. One has to maintain an 'image', an impression, status, role positioning; cover up weaknesses and act 'correct, perfect, pleasingly, respectfully, etc despite contradicting evidences.

6. There is a perpetual force to adopt the attitude of the group in order to maintain membership; eccentricities are humiliated and rejected - though unethical responses, behaviours, actions, and dialogues are tolerated. This paves the fear-and-anxiety to develop and maintain the centricity aspect [though non-conformity internally].

7. Several others also try for the limited resources and opportunities – survival of the fittest – so success is critical, and success against unknown population of unknown levels of competencies. This provides the logic for mental trap 3, namely fear-tension-anxiety about failure, future, etc. Their [parents-teachers-guides] comparisons, insults, intimidations, often ending up in the 'bad' dimension leads to the formation of the free-floating of 'low-ness', sensitivity to humiliation, criticisms, negative comments; development of improper self-images, inferiority feelings, or inferiority complex, etc. Such interfaces are filled with logics.

8. Environment, requirements, etc always changing: the nature of VUCA world provides logic for self-doubt and resource-myopia.

9. Campaigns about opportunities that are unclear and untrue or of chance, luck, 'connections', and such fortuitous aspects – leading to self-doubt and resource-myopia, inducing sense of meaninglessness, ennui, and disillusionment.

10. Stated and demanded requirement of 'doing' a job or work in the established ways and methods. As in the government offices and other regimented setting of activities. As well as 'learning' or developing 'knowing' about 'doing' and 'being'. Like the rigid and functionally fixed procedures-processes in schools and universities. This becomes the grounding for the mental trap of rigidity and functional fixedness. It gradually spreads like a virus to rigidity of expressions, responses, behaviours, actions, dialogues, work, and relationships.

11. The great majority of parents-teachers-guides try their best to make the child a duplicate entity of the statistics of collective consciousness. The so-called schooling is 97 per cent a design-setting-process for 'systematic desensitization' of the original engines of the body-mind-intellect-spirit of children.

12. Success orientation, compulsion for quick results, comparative achievement, 'time limits' for everything – learning, tests, exams, etc.

13. Intelligence traps are reinforced in the 'intelligent' students.

14. Campaigns of social-economic-religious 'state-of-being' and style of living etc contributing to the mental traps of familiarity trap, self-importance; quite paradoxically, in this land of Vedas and Upanishads of 'ayam-atma-brahma' and 'poornat-poornam udachyate'.

The mind-sets of responses, behaviours, actions, dialogues, etc that are initially adopted as a requirement to manage the above mentioned 'realities of the world' eventually become the dysfunctional mental traps.

The design and process of mental 'block' formation

The complex formation of mental traps is to be understood from different vantage points. See the following realities:

- Children are treated like pets and 'kids'. They are not allowed to understand on their own the consequences of failures before which the others or teachers intervene with judgments and conclusions and recommendations – mostly expressing negative energies. Even various forms of punishments and critiques are enforced. Extra activities are name-sake and make-belief, such as play, extra readings programs, and even learning of higher aesthetics such as dance, music, instruments, etc too are cut or restricted.

- Children are not permitted to formulate insights and cues from their own eccentricities and resultant experiences in expressions, responses, behaviours, dialogues, actions, and relationships. It could be relationships with events, entities, things, and phenomena in the nature. They are not allowed to delve into the mysteries of skies and stars, flowers and trees, the magic of birds, cats, and butterflies.

- Children are humiliated for their natural variations of expressions; their own experiments and observations are treated as negative eccentricities. They are forced rigorously to follow the established patterns of 'doings'. Everyone to sit in the class room and rote-learn, think, speak, and write about text-bookish kind of materials - exclusively.

- The teachers are rigorous representatives or agents of mental traps.

- Above all, the original sensitivities are de-linkaged. A vantage-point of self-respect is never inducted. Instead, items of self-importance based on evidences of the social, economic, caste positions and differences are supported.

- Even the so-called brilliant students of universities and higher learning centres are not inspired to develop any special responses, behaviours, dialogues, actions, and relationships; they are 'trapped' by the claims of 'knowing' - without any capacity-building for translating the 'knowings' into 'doings' and 'states-of-being'. In B-Schools, the exclusive focus is on the 'knowing'. Not on translating them into 'doing'. Not about the required or essential state of 'being' that defines the responses, actions, behaviours, work, relationships, of a manager or leader.

- By expansion and extreme penetration of modern media, especially the digital, coupled with various global campaign and open information about events and episodes all over the world, the mind has become overloaded with 'perceptions' - rather imposed perceptions. This induces what may be called 'free-floating anxiety', the 'familiarity trap', and the 'speed-trap'.

Tools, devices, and technologies have taken precedence over human beings. There is only a peripheral and transient pleasure in using high technologies but the 'flow' of mind, the processes of the body, the flow of the spirit are ever the same for the human species. As a result, the unconscious mind is very likely to feel 'wasted' or exhausted, defeated or belittled, and thereby the 'free-floating anxiety [actually considered a mild level of psychological problem]. As a result the tendency to needless or extra consumption of alcohol, drugs, tranquillizers, etc on ne side and a feeling of boredom and ennui, inability to feel the wonder and romance in relationships, and even increase in vulnerability to various 'process illnesses'.

All these in turn, add on to the already existent tendency of panic, anxiety, fear, apprehension etc of the parents, elders, peers, teachers, media, etc to use variety of 'languages' to induce mental blocks in children or to trigger and reinforce them in the population. The mental 'blocks' become empowered to the level of mental 'traps'.

What is 'blocked-prevented-rebuked' by the mental traps?

Of course, the blocked-prevented-rebuked is the great entelechies of creativity, originality, and genius.

The person is the mind. To the extent of 'I mind, therefore, I am'.
So, if there are mental traps, the person too is trapped.

The various engines-of-entity are ever ready to be trained or to be shaped to do anything probable-possible for them. All that great range of human activities and performances are the evidence. The entity carries the potentialities not only to enjoy music, rhythm, dance, colour and design variations; great ideas, performances, activities, etc, but also to do the 'doings' of them. But the 'mind' or the 'manager' of that entity is blocked to consider the possibility of trying only those 'doings' that are demonstrated, campaigned, and trained by the development environment.

In other words, the creature is capable and ready to sing, dance, paint, think, imagine, focus attention, reflection, dreaming, etc.
But the mind is not ready.

The self-image is not powerful and confident. Because, its original free-wheeling is trapped inside certain trained, duplicated, imposed mind-sets. The engines of the entity do the sensing of great lot of signals but they are not noticed by the mind and reflected upon by the intellect of the 'person'. There is no 'spirit' with the free-will of the person. There is no 'inspiration'. If at all, it is aborted by the mental traps even before it is fully conceived.

+++
Every rose is a rose is a rose. Every cat is a cat is a cat.
There are no nincompoop cats. Every nest constructed by the birds is firm, correct, elegant, taoic [in good 'flow'], and complete.

In fact, all other things, entities, and phenomena in the universe exist in or reach their completeness ['poornam'] of whatever they are created for. Of course, in their kind of 'knowing', 'doing', and 'being'.

Human species is considered the greatest form of living entities in the known universe. The sages and philosophers declare that human beings are made in the form of some supreme being called God or whatever. The supreme *Rishis* of ancient India talked about 'aham brahmasmi' and 'ayam-atma-brahma'. Mystics described the probable-possible spiritual development for accessing peak experience, enlightenment, and Satori almost as a birthright for every human being.

Then why it is not occurring-?
What else is blocking the individual other than something in his or her own mindberg, the 'mind-sets' that are imbibed from the environment, the contents of which are the only extra that is added onto the original entity.

Certainly those engines of the nature-process must have made every human entity a human entity the same way every cat is a cat. Firm-correct-elegant-taoic completeness in the translation of fertilized egg into a fully functioning organic assemblage. No human entity is made a lesser entity. Then why the so-called 'normal-distribution' of abilities for the human population-?

See, the human beings seldom reach the 'cat-ness' of the entity. Despite great facilities of language, knowledge domains, environment settings. Despite great 'knowings', institutions and systems that train all kinds of 'doings'. Despite perpetual messages about wisdom, evolution, and enlightenment delivered by deified gods and glorified sages and mystics. Legions of educated-intelligent people manifest clear inability to translate 'knowings' into corresponding 'doings' and 'states-of-being'. Why?

This lag for human beings is primarily due to mental traps.
The mental traps reduce the quality and completeness of expressions
or responses, behaviors, actions, and dialogues essential for effective
or creative job performance.   Severe mental traps induce negative and
dysfunctional emotions of envy and jealousy, greed and aggression,
prejudices and biases, hatred and anger, suicide and fratricide.

Mental traps hinder the motivation to develop the higher-order
entelechies or actualization of potentialities. Whatsoever be the desire
and drive for it. Ultimately, mental traps prevent the potentialities of
creativity, originality, and genius. Even the dedicated efforts for
self-realization, actualization, and enlightenment are waylaid
by the mental traps.

Mental Traps:
The Second Orbit of Linkages

Mental Traps and the Entelechy of Human Entities
Keyword: Entelechy

The term entelechy refers to 'the realization of potential',
'the actualization of form-giving cause', or 'the vital principle that guides
the development and functioning of an organism or other system or
organization'. The term also denotes the double process
of 'identifying' a potentiality and then 'developing' the same.

Every cat is a cat is a cat. There is no Normal Distribution Curve
applicable to cats and birds and fishes and amoebas and plants. Their
entelechy is firm, correct, elegant, complete, and taoic to provide all the
sensitivities and methods of functions and actions required for
survival-sustenance.

Unlike cats and birds, the human beings have to discover or create and
learn the required expressions of entelechy. As the human entities are
provided with the greatest range of potentialities [entelechies], there is
the requirement of realising, actualising, and mastering their expressions
and manifestations. They have created new settings and processes in the
spaces of nature. In the nature there are no buildings of any kind, no
cultivation. No businesses, no trade, no manufacturing organizations, no
universities, no philosophies-sciences and technologies. The quality of
survival-sustenance in a complex man-created world would depend upon
the extent of entelechy achieved by an individual, or organization, or any
of the man-created entity, thing, phenomenon.

The mental traps affect self-development and entelechy in several ways:

- The mind is full of mind-sets. The mental traps too are
  mind-sets; but carry the power of driving, neutralizing, or
  suppressing 'other' mind-sets. For instance, a person is capable
  of singing, but the mind-set [or the mental block of anxiety of
  comparison would suppress the inspiration to sing on the stage].

The mental blocks operate very creatively in restricting the firm-correct-elegant-taoic completeness of responses, behaviours, actions, and dialogues and life-work-relationships.

- The blocking mind-sets operate so creatively, that most of the time the person might not be aware of them. The blocking mind-sets may work even during sleep and reflect in the dreams.
- Life and survival-sustenance involve the interactions of immense varieties of situations and contexts where the individual must express himself, respond to others, behave, act, talk, cooperate, and so on.
- So, the mind-sets of mental blocks-traps also would be triggered in such interactions. For instance, did you ever try to dance, participate in drama or other performance arts, music, musical instruments, drawing, painting, craft-works; poetry, short story, diary writing; operating mechanical-electrical tools, repairing things; cooking, gardening, hiking, mountaineering, cycling, or any one or more of the so-called extra-curricular activities-? If not, why?

  - Due to anxiety and fear of unknown-strange-new; ambiguous-uncertain-unexpected-etc?
  - Is it to due to anxiety of failure, humiliation, comparison, feeling insecure, or sensing danger?
  - Is it due to centricity-conformity [majority is not 'doing' it, though] the majority is going to temples because the majority is going..?

Be firmly clear about the primary setting of the mind.
The mind is a process and product at the same time. So, the mind assumes the decisive role of driving itself. A trapped mind drives itself in trapping methods. Like a tense novice driver of a powerful engine on a road of heavy traffic.

A so-called ignorant mind manages itself in an ignorant way.
Of course, a creative mind drives itself in a creative way.

The Second Orbit of Mental Trap 1: Fear, tension, panic, anxiety about the ambiguous, uncertain, strange, unexpected, new, unfamiliar, etc

The second orbit of this mental trap would be mild in linkages. Because, the various systems and procedures established in the environment [government, institutions, arrangements, policies, norms, rules, etc] ensure a more or less 'clear' operating environment. There is normally no compulsion for 'knowing' or 'doing' any unknown, unclear, ambiguous, new things. If at all, there would be a team or group to cooperate in such activities.

In other words, the ambiguities and unclear things, new etc in the 'external environment' can be avoided to a great extent [regardless of whatever VUCA]. But, if new and unclear and ambiguous and unexpected things happen in the 'internal world' [of body, mind, intellect, intelligence, spirit], then they cannot be 'avoided'. State of vague pains, upsets of body conditions, undue illnesses, etc of the body cannot be easily understood and avoided. No quick-fix techniques and guides may be available or effective if vague and free-floating anxiety captures the mind; no amount of counter-thoughts may resolve a depressing, defeating thought or idea to commit unethical and antisocial acts and behaviours. Most of the crimes are culminated despite clear disagreement from within.

That is why most criminals 'deny' their role in a crime. They wonder themselves, albeit secretly, how they could 'talk violence', how they could do, or perpetrate crimes and manipulations of various kinds..!

'Growth and Development' in Mental Trap of Fear, Tension, and Anxiety of Unknown, Uncertain, etc
Children are protected from all kinds of unfamiliar things and experiences, living most of their times in safe secure predictable settings. As a result, they will become victims of this mental trap in their future times of increasing alienation and undependable and ambiguous relationships.

Please analyze the table below showing the mean scores of respondents chosen from two time-spans. The highest increase revealed is in the mental trap of fear-tension-anxiety of ambiguity, uncertainty, etc. [Indicated by the difference in the percentages of the Mean and Standard Deviation].

Table 8: Data Means of two time periods [1992-2001 to 2006-2016]
[Differentiated from the data of the 'larger sample' of N: 13,365]

	MS1	MS2	MS3	MS4	MS5	MS6	MS7
2006-2016 [N: 1,341]	56%	52%	47%	41%	38%	48%	48%
1992-2001 [N: 8,194]	48%	51%	42%	35%	38%	46%	45%
SD 2006-2016	13%	12%	13%	14%	14%	11%	10%
SD 1992-2001	16%	13%	14%	13%	15%	13%	9%

Note: The data collected in between the years of 2001 and 2004 is omitted to highlight difference in the mean scores of two time-spaces. That is, the data of a sample of N: 8,880 is omitted - in the table above.

Schooling and the fear of ambiguity ...

The great tragedy in the drama of 'Schooling' [as well as 'Colleging']: Instead of training the intellect competencies [of observation, analysis, thinking, projection, reflection, etc], schooling is a core and powerful coaching centre for mental traps. The highest mental trap of teachers is the fear-anxiety of unknown, ambiguous, unclear, new, strange, unexpected, etc. Text books are all 'completely clear, definite, precise.

Table 9 given next indicates the average mental traps of teachers in Schools [Secondary and Plus-2 level] and Colleges. Out of the total sample of 451 teachers, not a single respondent had all the mental traps in the acceptable 'threshold' range [below 19%]. And, they are in charge of guiding and developing confidence and personality of children, developing the talents and specialities of children who are entrusted in them for 10-12 years ..!

It is the greatest tragedy of the genius-loci of Indian education design-setting-process.

	MS1	MS2	MS3	MS4	MS5	MS6	MS7
School Teachers							
[N: 331]	**53%**	42%	41%	52%	30%	40%	42%
College Teachers							
[N: 90]	**39%**	31%	33%	26%	24%	34%	33%

Importance and significance attached to art, literature, music, poetry, NCC, Scouts, and such extra-curricular activities' are almost absent in a great number of schools. It should be made compulsory. For, they are all about 'doing' and 'being'. These kind of doings will reduce some of the mental traps to a great extent. Perhaps, the climate and culture perpetuated by female teachers do not support an environment for the freedom of extra-curricular activities.

The Second Orbit of Mental Trap 2: Centricity-Conformity
The first set of mind-sets induced in a child

There is a logic about why centricity and conformity is induced in the little child.

First of all, the little child has no language. So the child has to imitate or approximate his expressions, responses, actions, etc according to the 'models' in front.

Second of all, the very physical surrounding insists or compels the developing child to abide by certain behaviours, actions, responses. If someone is sitting on the only one chair in a room, the other person has to stand. Eating is possible only when the food is ready. Dress has to be removed before taking the bath. Kitchen is located after the dining hall.

Third of all, the people setting around would invariably intervene in the learning-development curriculum of the child. Almost every adult who comes across a child would induce one or the other form of block.

Human beings can do expressions responses-behaviors-actions-dialogues and relationships only according to what they 'know or can do and be'. But, what comprises the so-called knowledge and 'knowing' of the majority of people? Mostly, duplicated and rote-learned items only. The 'knowings' are not reflected upon, analysed and thereby made 'original' for the self one's own ['internalization or originalization' of learning]. Therefore, the expressions, responses, behaviors, dialogues, and actions and relationships would tend to look alike in a given time-space-location. This is centricity-conformity. Thus, the mind-set of centricity-conformity works the core engine of socialization, social adaptation, or social intelligence.

For instance, after interacting with a guru or learning of great ideologies such as in spiritual texts, etc the self or its expressions, responses, behaviors, dialogues, and actions; work and relationships tend to remain more or less the same as ever before. It is due to the mental trap of centricity-conformity.

In other words, despite 'knowings' [and even 'doings'], the 'being' remains the same. Because, the self is in centricity-conformity with the contents of the memory and experience, despite changed life conditions and new perspectives. Despite external conformity and centricity with high-tech gadgets and tools, knowings and ideologies the interior world would continue to carry the attitudes of prejudices and biases of 'double-standards'. of various kinds and categories.

India is a typical example of such double standards due to mental traps. Of course, all weaknesses are generated by the mental traps only.

It is very likely that the deities or the gurus are worshipped due to centricity. Because, they were discerned by supreme sensitivities of genius level individuals. Seldom the ideas related to those deities are actual-ised in the self and lived. Because, the self becomes sort of inescapably trapped in its salient or most used ways due to decades of live 'duplication' of mental taps about the very self. Division and separation cannot exist just outside. It penetrates into the insides too: a 'divided self'.

People do not verify or try to know firmly-clearly why a certain social class is to be treated with a 'low-attitude'; why a caste is to be seen as 'low', why some other caste is treated as high, etc.

Instead, people simply imitate the expressions behaviors etc that are manifested by the social-network or group or sensed from the 'collective consciousness' expressed, in news, events, media, traditions, practices, and so on. By centricity-conformity majority of populations in India treat the so-called third gender with disdain and abandonment. Even the Judiciary is confused about 'gender' issues.

The mind-sets of 'centricities and conformities' are induced rather straight. The parents may openly suggest, enforce, command, the expressions, responses, behaviors, actions, dialogues, work, and relationships according to 'centricities and conformities' specified for situations, people, events, settings, ideologies, principles, values, attitudes, etc.

Satyam-eva Jayate and hundreds of such Sutras tend to remain as 'knowings'. Not as 'doings' or 'states-of-being'. Evidence is the history, past, and present. Of course, all due to mental traps and mental traps only. What else can stop the 'doings' of such marvellous great perspectives?

See the differentiation and subtle [and some times open] division-separation of castes, sub-castes, communities, etc in India. Why not any consideration of the 'truth' of human entity-ness that unites the entire species? When so-called 'scientific truths' are glamorized and compulsively adhered to in perception, thinking, activities, and all such foundation of the current world, why that truth of human entities is abandoned? If so much obsessed about centricity and conformity, why not to the great engines of the entity, the greatest of known species?

Great centricity-conformity to 'knowings'. Yet, no 'doing' of those 'knowing'. As a result, the 'being' remains oblivious to its own genius. Jesus did his 'doing'. Buddha suggested the right paths.

But the dedicated entities of Jesus or Buddha do not seem to do such quality and completeness in their 'doings'.

Conformity can be based on solid or firm clear understanding of a 'knowing' or 'rational scientific ideas'. But the believing aspect or 'belief' itself is carried in the caskets of mental traps. Induced by rigorous teaching, guiding, modelling, etc or willingly duplicated, imitated, adopted for mere centricity-conformity. For instance, religious conversions, political conversions, changing participation in groups and social-networks, etc.

	MS1	MS2	MS3	MS4	MS5	MS6	MS7
MALE Disciples-Visitors [N: 75]	60%	52%	41%	40%	41%	49%	51%
FEMALE Disciples-Visitors [N: 90]	64%	53%	55%	45%	40%	58%	53%
Theosophical Seminary, Kerala [Trainee Priests] [N:65]	45%	41%	36%	31%	26%	41%	39%

7

Above all, centricity-conformity induces stronger internal or psychological linkages. The individual tends to be centred in his or her own limited 'knowing' whatever learning and experience, duplicated responses, behaviors-actions and dialoguing patterns [altogether forming the self of the person]. Also the ways of body activities, mental transactions, ways of thinking, etc too become affected by the mind-sets of 'centricity-conformity'.

8

The individual becomes a victim trapped into the territories of internal centricity-conformity. The self-image, self-description, and self-perception become trapped in the available ways of 'doing' and familiar 'states-of-being'. As a result, the continuity of evolution is blocked.

9

If the individual feels or thinks stupid or sorry about one's own self, then such a self becomes a sorry self, a depressed self, a weak self.

That is inner centricity. The methods of 'self-affirmations' is an antidote for such negative or weak self image. In other words, the individual conforms to the thoughts about oneself – as good or bad, right or wrong, correct or incorrect, small or great, creative or non-creative, original or duplicated stupid or genius.

10

The core of every item of learning-development is in the mind-setting of centricity-conformity. The disciple or student or learner has to clearly and completely be centred in the responses-behaviors-actions suggested and conform to the discipline and guidelines proposed by the guru or master or trainer. This is an advantage of the mind-setting of centricity-conformity.

11

By external centricity-conformity, individuals adapt to the society and its systems-processes-procedures: forming of the 'social being'. But as a consequence, the intellect develops the strong tendency to go by the perceptions, views, experiences, etc that occur inside about the available and relatively easier path of survival-sustenance and existence.

Teachers report that the ongoing generation of students or learners are disinterested in reading, developing life skills, various competencies essential for the future, etc. There is a craving for quick-work 'techniques' than mastery of methods for long-range applications. Examinations have become peripheral by ticking answers out of 'multiple choices'.

In the modern schooling learning is positioned as 'fun'. By centricity-conformity all 'doings' are duplicated in mechanical ways - imitated carelessly. As a result even the highest goals of existence too become blocked. The futuristic 'fictions' by Isaac Asimov are likely to come real.

12

Centricity-Conformity blocks spiritual enlightenment or Satori.

The way individuals adapt with the external world by centricity-conformity, they get adapted to the statistical means of 'personal history', instead of the greater than +3 Sigma points in one's life.

Being trapped in the easy or non-challenging levels of 'knowing' and 'doing' contaminates the power of the engines-of-intellect to see the reflection and the reflected realities - outside and inside.

Centricity-conformity: A paradox

Actually, all the mind-sets that become mental traps are inherently paradoxical. Because, all those mind-sets are absolutely essential or necessary at threshold levels and all those mind-sets become dysfunctional and disadvantageous if they are beyond the threshold levels [medium-high-serious mental traps].

Out of all the 9 mind-sets, the mental trap of centricity-conformity is the most paradoxical. On one side, the teachers, leaders, parents, public figures, etc insist on conformity to good character, values, ethics, and related ideologies of greatness. But on the other side, their own centricities may end up in evidences of corruption, bribery, various forms of manipulation, cunningness, etc.

By insisting conformity, a good number of people just learn the lessons of the required behaviour without originalizing them on one side; yet violating rules and regulations normally required for survival and sustenance and various official works, on the other. By such duplication of norms, the power of original decision-making is affected. Some children would quickly realize that just agreeing to the instructions is the easy way. So, during the late childhood and early adult stages, they continue that pretension and when opportunity comes they tend to join the unethical and fraudulent people and practices – as seen all over the world.

Someone who understands [conformity] the reality and validity of temple rituals may never even visit [centricity[a temple. And those who does not understand anything about it [no conformity] may be regular visitors [centricity]. A nonconformist in views about marriage ceremonies may agree for a highly elaborate set of rituals. Anyone can differentiate plenty of manifestations of such paradox of mental traps if events and people around and reported in media are reflected upon for a minute.
In this mental-block of centricity-conformity, there is often an 'agreement' or even public surrender or declared followership.
At the same time, there may not be an agreement for centricity [expected, responses, behaviors-actions-dialogues] driven expressions.

But there can be openly accepted, declared, pledged agreement in most of the conformities. Certain religions demand public declaration of such agreements to the 'knowings' without any reference to the 'doing' of them. This is a paradox. By centricity-conformity, even the drive for self-actualization [a clearly personal secret journey] ends up influenced by public acceptance and recognition. An individual's competencies in some domains are convincing for the public only by the mark of rewards and awards. Great majority of Indian geniuses have been accepted and recognised only after they were noticed by the 'powerful' western sources. The success and achievement of 'others' are treated with disdain or disregard. Happy about the defeat and failure of others on one side and wide campaign for success and achievement.

India is a tragic case of heavy mental trap of centricity and conformity. Evidences are plenty, everywhere. The 'required threshold block' of centricity-conformity often tends to evolve into high and severe disadvantages under conditions of:

- inappropriate level of self-image or self-perception
- a 'state-of-being' driven by the non-conscious stack of mental-block mind-sets and impressions recorded thereof along with corresponding quality, impact, completeness of the 'doings'
- artificial, duplicated, pretentious 'behaviors, actions, dialogues, relationships, work, etc
- competition driven by comparison and rivalry
- duplicated identity, conflict of identity leading to depression
- change in allegiance to change in sources of power
- even children disowning parents, separation or disdain for spouses, choice of social network, vilification campaigns etc by reasons of variations in social, economic, role status
- feeling 'bad' about oneself or associates [based on standards of centricity prevailing in the culture, location, milieu, etc]
- disregard and contempt and exclusion of the poor and disadvantaged; lower strata of employees, workers, etc. and so on ...

Centricity-Conformity and the 'trust-distrust factor'

Ideally, the required mind-sets of centricity and conformity are to be driven by a core mind-set of 'trust'. The beginning of a child is by that trust factor. Trust in the guru-daivam-ness of parents. The child starts with the complete trust in the parents and there may be several instances, events, episodes, dialogues, etc that may provide evidences to the child that they are not trustworthy. However, the child continues to conform to them despite the lack of trust because of its helplessness and dependence.

Later, the majority leaders, powerful others, etc too are conformed to or followed in the same way - without any real trust in them. However, the social, religious, political kind of leaders try their best strategies to define and derive the trust of populations. Often to shift the trust from one to the other. The democratic election campaigns are a typical example.
In the very process of teaching-training-guiding the child is treated with an energy-field of distrust. The same distrust about the child's ability to manage the environment is applied in its ability to learn the norms, rules, and regulations.

The human grounding of survival-sustenance depends mostly on human beings themselves – unlike all other beings. They have to be 'socially adaptable, cooperating, ethical', and not to injure and intimidate other human beings. Every child is liable to discover this reality, more-or-less the way it formed the 'ego' by the process of 'reality testing'. But, by forced induction into norms which conceals a doubt in the inherent truth of the entity, the person loses his natural credit of integrity and ethics. For, the flow of life is individual specific and there cannot be any general rule for individual-specific situations.

So, the pretenders feel the freedom to violate rules when some others who are more convinced about their rebellion apply pressure. They too join the gang for the secret thrill and happiness of revolting against the authority and cheating the 'system'. Those who suppressed their revolt against the very parents would find it comfortable and convenient to violate the system.

Eccentricity and the mental trap of centricity-conformity

However, eccentricity is not at all against norms. In the eccentric
world-view, any view is a probable-possible view. Any view of the
majority too is right. But just one of the rights. Any vantage point is only
one of the vantage points. Like a vantage point: that, any human entity is
only one of the species.

Eccentricity is not against law and order or norms and rules and
regulations, culture and traditions. But the eccentrics may not follow
them blindly. They are not against the mediocre and silly. In fact they
are more tolerant to mediocrity. Whereas mediocrity is not tolerant
towards mediocrity. That is why everyone is blaming and criticising the
other. Thus, compared to the eccentrics, the life of the mediocrity is very
troublesome.

So, in the world, those who carry high mental traps of centricity
and conformity create all problems of unethical and anti-existential.
Intimidating, injuring, offending anyone else is nothing but a direct
expression of high-to-severe mental traps only. What else?

Only controlled-eccentricity can help managing survival and
happiness in the current and future ambiguous, uncertain, testing world.
A world increasingly trapped by the trinity of rulers-clerics-traders.
For, eccentricity is resilience, eccentricity is freedom from defeats of
the self. Eccentricity is flexibility and ensure the power of 'variation'.
Eccentricity only can lead to the attendant spirit, and eccentricity only
can assist entry through the gate-less gate to Satori.

So, don't be compulsive about the plans and planning about life, work,
and relationships. Don't be obsessed about the possibility of a peaceful,
great, beautiful world of events and people and phenomena. Create your
beautiful world around you. The reality is where you are really positioned.
Your people, your friends, your space and neighbourhood, your work and
your relationships.

When the mental trapped leaders-managers of some nations want to feel confident about their mindbergs and locus of control, they would intimidate other nations. And the unsuspecting population of that nation would be forced to abide by enforced centricities and conformities; despite their strong realizations contrary to those of the leaders-managers. For, their mindbergs too are trapped in mental traps. Therefore, it may be said that, the world is but a live film where mental traps direct the lead roles.

Reportedly, Michael Nostradamus said about the future:
'People with psychological power will survive'.
The greatest source of Psychological power: freedom from fear-anxiety-tension. The populations may have to survive in the increasingly difficult and complex consequences of supreme forms of corruption and evil in many critical aspects of survival and sustenance systems, processes, and procedures.

Centricity-Conformity leading to 'Taken-for-Granted' attitude about existence

By centricity-conformity, the very entity is 'taken-for-granted'.
A lot of young educated people suppress their inspirations or new knowing, because of centricity-conformity due to the following linkages:

1
The duplicated mind-setting that all knowing is for some purpose, or for some benefit and advantage, though the very schooling in various subjects serve no purpose for individual learners. If one subject is finally chosen, learning in the other subjects or developing knowledge for the sake of it is considered a waste of time.
2
The obsession [duplicated] that one's knowings should be recognized by others, at least by the social-network. This is duplication, that when one's earnings and possessions are kept personal and for private use, the learning and knowing should get public attention and recognition…!

3

Great part of expressions, responses, behaviours, and activities are introduced to the developing child from an 'others perspective'. This too is a predicament of the developing child that he or she does not become interested and inspired in the type and kind of knowing and doing and being vis-a-vis the 'syllabus'. In the hurry and impatience of quickly finishing the job of training the child, the social-setting wants to enforce centricity and conformity by referring to punitive public forces or primitive personal forces and consequences thereof.

The developing child does not become inspired in his knowing and doing and being. Or whatever that inspired the child is not given support and 'holding environment'.

4

The child is forcibly trained to duplicate the perception and learn from the reported experience of others that any learning or ways of doing etc are not possible without the support and guidance of the 'others': teachers, elders, or class rooms, etc. Genuine self-learners are sort of side-lined by labelling them 'autodidacts'. Of course, most people find it difficult to self-learn a 'new' field of knowledge or new type of doing. As a result, campaigns of 'continuous learning' fall into closed ears.

In the decades of schooling, the learners are not trained in the ways and powers of intellect-engines. As a result, they cannot construct any new knowing or doing or state-of-being even when they become interested later. Finding difficulty in new learning, they feel the mental trap of lowness or fear of new and challenging things and abandon the inspirations.

Learning a few subjects, developing competencies to do some doings and then proceed to 'live' and work with those basic qualifications is very similar to sub-human creatures. Of course, there is nothing wrong about that. This is what even the primitive people did. The tools and terrains of knowing and doing are just mechanically different from those times.

Individuals need to reconsider their intents and perspectives about knowledge and development. Individuals need to understand the basic design of human entities. That they are not like sub-human creatures that develop all that they can and then continue to manage their survival and sustenance. Perhaps, the very purpose of having such powerful central nervous system and free-wheeling engines of the mindberg and free-floating engines-of-intellect are for that ever-continuous process of 'knowing' and 'doing' new activities and then discovering the ultimate moment of Satori.

5

Centricity-conformity: Taking the entity too for granted.

The core mind-set of centricity has to be designed out of fear-tension-anxiety about future, about consequences of actions, about possible-probable failures and insecurities etc. Because, the basic motive force of human entities are around survival sustenance – which is always in uncertainty and ambiguity.

What you can see in the Indian environment is the 'taken-for-granted' attitude. Contempt towards and-or disregard for a lot of things Indian.

The essentiality of centricity-conformity

Conformity and centricity is 'programmed' in the very design-setting of the nature-process. In every species. For instance, human entities must conform to the nature-processes. Both outside and within. If hunger, one has to eat. One has to defecate whether president of the world or guru of humanity, evil or good, man or woman, landlord or servant, child or old aged.

Of course, without threshold centricity-conformity life or survival and sustenance or coexistence itself is impossible. Therefore, the governance institutions, organizations, groups, family heads, elders, leaders; traders, clerics, rulers etc are all the top engines of society that drive populations into centricity-conformity.

The Second Orbit of Mental Trap 3: Fear-Tension-Anxiety of failure, defeat, loss, negative future, tight-tough routine, etc.

There can be the fear, or anxiety, or tension of anticipated failure in work or 'tests and examinations'; or loss of love, to finish an assignment on time, anticipated delay in meeting targets, to reach an important location on time, etc. Such 'free-floating anxieties' will induce various psychosomatic illnesses: diabetes, tension-headaches, increased blood pressure, digestive disorders, fatigue, etc.

Several interviews provided evidence that individuals who are calm, cool, and composed in any challenging situation carry no trace of mental traps. Individuals who were trained in transcending mental traps reported amazing ways of managing their extremely complex work and difficult relationships, as well as being treated by colleagues as role-models and sought after for guidance and inspiration. Top management hand-picked them regardless of seniorities and entrusted them with assignment that were difficult for others or mismanaged by even highly experienced managers.

The Second Orbit of Mental Trap 4: The complex mental trap of fear-tension-anxiety of 'humiliation and comparison', 'low-ness', and 'inferiority complex'

There is fear-tension-anxiety about the possible-probable occurrence of fear-tension-anxiety itself. Fear of being afraid. For instance, someone who is getting more and more powerful role positions may develop fear-tension-anxiety about losing it or some parallel damage elsewhere in work or life or relationships. There is even the supportive axiom that, 'no gain without loss'.

Someone from the 'low' of hierarchies would sense certain anxiety by anticipating 'subdued treatment' from 'high' others. High side of populations seldom interact with the 'low' side due to anxiety of 'low-ness' anticipated [for obvious reasons].

Even close relatives, siblings, and parents are placed into oblivion by the 'high' due to the anticipatory fear-and-anxiety of 'low-ness'. In that sense, everyone is sensitive to the mental traps and is a victim and therefore constantly try to drive their survival and sustenance and responses, behaviours, and actions, work and relationships in a tight traffic of mental traps.

Fear-tension-anxiety of 'low-ness' versus 'high-ness'

As a result of this mental trap, people tend to disregard people, events, entities, things, and phenomena that are considered, valued low; disregard and side-lining populations of human beings; the certain classes and castes are sort of ostracized and regarded untouchables. Even now 'honor killings' is an honour.

From the vantage point of individual evolution, or enlightenment and Satori, the advantageous path is blocked because of the tendency of disregarding the simple and the small of the 'details'. People are not able to trust that the 'God is in the details' because the so-called details are so silly and simple and negligible: LOW

Rabindranath Tagore, in his Gitanjali declared: "God is there where the tiller is tilling the hard ground and the path maker is making the path..." Some of the human beings work for constructing the roads and bridges and buildings, working irrigation and cultivating and mending farmlands. Builds dams and temples and monuments and houses of all kinds. The masons, carpenters, locksmiths, shepherds, plumbers, and so on. They work in the lowest of shop-floors, scavengers, cleaners, janitors, and cooks and caretakers of children. Teachers of lower primary school are lower than those in higher-secondary and so on.

> How come in the Aham Brahmasmi land of India there is such obsessive attention and extra-linkages about 'low-ness' of humans? Low is low and high is high. Let it be. Let the head of Brahma be greater than his feet. So what? How the human species are formed? How come negative temperament and injurious attitude based on the type of work for survival sustenance?

If the work of a person is unknown then this high-low attitude is less forceful. There are countless theories and explanations about the uniquely powerful phenomena that has destroyed the genius of this land. However, we want to point out evidences that almost every human being is but a 'worker'. Driven by the motivation hierarchy.

At the technology 'farmlands', the juniors are working for seniors, and then to super seniors, and finally the top management work for the owners. Then the owners work for whom? The *pujaris* work for whom? The mystics and gurus work for whom? The details of the very planet Earth work for whom? For what?

Thus, behind most of the mental traps, especially of 'low-ness' [the mental trap that interferes with virtually every social process in India] there is the absolute missing engines of intellect, lack of wider perspective, wisdom and understanding about existence, lack of clarity in the belief in religion or gods and deities, unclear identity [not self-image, which can be based on purely external factors with absolute conflict in identity] and a thick veil of sensitivity-lag. A terrible lack of 'creative sensitivity'.

Thirdly, because of the disregard for the small and the little and therefore taken   unimportant; the focus on creativity, innovation, and discovery is the lowest in this country for the last thousands of years. Because of the mental trap of 'low-ness', the genius and originality of 'others' is sidelined in India. Almost every genius individual of India has been recognised by the people in other countries.

As a result of this mental trap, the rulers, clerics, traders, and the great educated intelligent population do not look at the solitary reapers and falling apples and overflowing waters in their own land. Perhaps, within them too. Thus the mental trap of fear-tension-anxiety of 'low-ness' and humiliation is the most vicious among all mental traps:

- it governs 'conspicuous consumption' - to manage or compensate low-ness and-or to sustain high-ness,

- it governs the 'mental economy': biasing the expressions, responses, behaviors, dialogues, and actions; work and relationships of people,
- it governs the social-economic-cultural-political environment of a location.

'Low-ness' and Inferiority Complex

From the vantage point of Clinical Psychology, this fear-tension-anxiety of 'low-ness' directly induces 'inferiority feelings'. It is a mental block by itself. But when the mental trap of 'low-ness' is 'high' then the inferiority 'feelings' give shape to 'inferiority complex*' – which is a dysfunctional state. Though dysfunctional in its core, it can drive some people to great achievement also - as a 'compensation'.

> ***Inferiority complex is due to a secret but clear sense of lack of self-worth, a doubt and uncertainty about oneself, and feelings of not measuring up to standards. It is often subconscious, and is thought to drive afflicted individuals to overcompensate, resulting either in spectacular achievement or extremely asocial or antisocial-criminal and unethical behavior, actions, and relationships [especially marital relationships].

According to Alfred Adler, a genius psychologist:
> "Our idea of social feeling as the final form of humanity - of an imagined state in which all the problems of life are solved and all our relations to the external world rightly adjusted - is a regulative ideal, a goal that gives our direction. This goal of perfection must bear within it the goal of an ideal community, because all that we value in life, all that endures and continues to endure, is eternally the product of this social feeling."***

***Social Interest: A Challenge to Mankind, Alfred Adler, 1938, translated by Linton John, Richard Vaughan, pp. 275–276

By the classical Adlerian psychology there are primary and secondary inferiority feelings:

1. The primary inferiority feeling is said to be rooted in the young child's original experience of weakness, helplessness, and dependency. It can then be intensified by the ways of teaching-training-guiding offered by the parents and others, environment, etc. Often it is induced by comparisons to siblings, romantic partners, and other relevant entities of power and esteem.
2. The secondary inferiority feeling relates to an adult's experience of being unable to reach a 'reassuring fictional final goal of subjective security and success' to compensate for the inferiority feelings.
3. The perceived distance from that reassuring goal would lead to a negative feeling or depression that could then prompt the recall of the original inferiority feeling [this composite of inferiority feelings could be very strong driver of emotions, nature and quality of expressions, responses, behaviors, dialogues, and actions, and relationships].

The reassuring goal invented to relieve the original, primary feeling of inferiority which actually causes the secondary feeling of inferiority is the "catch-22" of this dilemma, where the desperate attempt to obtain therapeutic reassurance and delivery from a depressing feeling of inferiority and worthlessness repeatedly fails. This vicious cycle is common in neurotic lifestyles.

The popular concept of 'superiority complex' is the outcome of a unique set of psychological defense mechanisms in which a person's pretensions of superiority counter or conceal his or her feelings of inferiorities.

The 'logic' of development of inferiority-feeling
As in the case of other mental-blocks, the fear-tension-anxiety of 'low-ness' or inferiority-feeling too is induced during early development times. Of course, that time can extend sporadically to adult stages also. But the roots are linkaged in the early years especially at home, peer groups, and greatly strong during schooling.

The 'inferiority complex' occurs when the feelings of inferiority are intensified in the individual through discouragement or failure, negative comparison, sidelining, abandonment, etc. Children reared in households where they were constantly criticized or did not live up to parents' expectations may also develop an inferiority complex. Many times there are warning signs to someone who may be more prone to developing an inferiority complex. For example, someone who is prone to attention and approval-seeking behaviors may be more susceptible.

Also, inferiority feeling results when adults feel inadequate from desires to achieve unobtainable or unrealistic results, thwarted achievement, etc. Stresses associated with feelings of failure and inferiority cause a pessimistic attitude and an inability to overcome difficulties in life. Individuals with high inferiority-feeling tend to manifest signs of low self-esteem or self-worth, have a history of depression symptoms, and often belong to low socio-economic status. However, as in all other mental-blocks, certain threshold level of inferiority-feeling may drive genuine growth and development, achievements.

According to Alfred Adler:
> "Everyone (...) has a feeling of inferiority. But the feeling of inferiority is not a disease; it is rather a stimulant to healthy, normal striving and development. It becomes a pathological condition only when the sense of inadequacy overwhelms the individual and, far from stimulating him to useful activity, makes him depressed and incapable of development."
> [Details can be known from any book on the 'Theories of Personality'].

'Low-ness', Inferiority-complex and inter-personal relationships

In the corporate culture of India, driven by so much of mental traps [as revealed in the 23+ year longitudinal study behind this book] even work out put depends upon relationships. Of course, the very design-setting-process of existence, the very requirements of survival-sustenance can be managed only by relationships.

Relationships that induce inferiority-feeling cannot continue for long in any advantageous way. In other words, people of more or less same level of inferiority-feeling would tend to form their social-network. This is the common process with all other mental traps also. However, this mental trap is more complicated due to its 'social base'. If there are no 'others' there is no ground for inferiority-feeling or fear-tension-anxiety of 'low-ness'.

In the so-called 'advanced' west, a huge population of human beings are labelled and referred-to as 'blacks'. In India, a great number of adolescents are carrying anxiety and depression about their 'dark complexion'. The most-sold cosmetic item in the country is that of complexion enhancement. The evidence of body inferiority-feeling includes the embarrassment in making 'non-usual movements' such as in dance, theatre, sports-games, etc.

Inferiority 'Feeling' and Appreciation
Surprising that only about 3 out of about 70-75 people could really 'take' an act or dialogue of appreciation in a 'cool' way or confident way. The instant reaction is one of rejecting, or humble dishonouring 'Oh no, it is all a coincidence, not so great about me' etc. Rarely anyone said even a 'thank you'. Whereas, even the slightest trace of criticism or negative comment was taken 'seriously'. On the other side, people with inferiority complex cannot appreciate the high performance or achievement of others.

Strategies to transcend inferiority-feelings
- Develop wisdom and understanding about existence
- Analyze the variant-invariant-orbit-linkage-intent-network of any identified or possible-probable inferiority-feelings
- Development the Zen-Mind

The Zen-Mind may be facilitated by training in:
- Analytic intellection
- Ensuring free-wheeling-ness of mind
- Developing creative-language-control

Fear-and-anxiety of 'low-ness' and work
When an inferiority complex is in full effect, it may impact the performance of an individual as well as impact an individual' self-esteem. Individuals suffering from inferiorities do not ensure that their own outputs of responses-behaviors-actions-dialogues work relationships are of 'superior quality'. On the other hand, people suffering inferiority tend to behave bad-wrong-incorrect, unethical negative, dysfunctional, etc.

The logic of the above process [that inferior begets inferior] is evidenced thus: if a person is known for the quality and competency of his work, then his mental-block of fear-and-anxiety of 'low-ness' would be low or threshold level. Because, he or she already feel 'compensated' for the sensed level of inferiority feelings or have never experienced inferiority.

This inferiority-feeling may carry linkages with other mental-blocks such as self-doubt or resource myopia, rigidity, and self-importance [lack of 'self-respect'].

There needs to be clearly defined training programs for resolving 'inferiority complex' that corrupts the mind-setting of a great majority of 'Corporate Indians'. Especially in the government and public administration services.

Institutions, organizations, etc. A hierarchy of 'low-ness'?
Or a hierarchy of 'high-ness'?
The type of work is classified and the people who do that work are also classified. A Vice President is 'lower' than Chief Executive Officer. Ministers are all 'lower' than the Prime Minister. The wife is considered 'lower'. Woman 'lower' than man. What is 'wrong or bad' with low? Why the 'low' is seen or perceived with a depreciation and derogation if not clear avoidance and sidelining, even subjected to of violence and killing and annihilating?

The fact: human beings are working class - all sort of 'sudraas' - working for the making of the world. Working for the continuity of existence process of the species.

Fear, Tension, and Anxiety of 'High-ness'
[the loss of 'high' position, money, reputation, etc]
As a paradox of the mental process, certain fear and anxiety of 'high-ness' too is possible-probable for a good majority of managers and leaders. The dynamics involves more or less same as that of mental traps. Because, role positions of high authority and power, decisions on money and people can induce a sense of 'heavy challenge' and the anxiety of failure and uncertainty linkaged to it. A good number of people in high positions in institutions, organizations, and governance are likely to have this mental trap and manifesting maladjusted patterns of responses, behaviours, actions, dialogues, work, and relationships. Psychological research has identified such maladjusted patterns in leaders. They are named 'Toxic Leaders'.

THE TOXIC LEADERS:

Based on empirical research, Kathie L. Pelletier identified certain behavioural characteristics of 'Toxic Leaders' as follows:

- Attack on followers' self esteem: by demeaning, marginalising, or degrading; ridiculing, mocking
- Lack of integrity: being deceptive, blaming others for leader's mistakes, bending the rules to meet goals
- Abusiveness: Displaying anger, emotional volatility, coercing

- Excluding individuals from social functions
- Divisiveness: ostracising employee, inciting employee to chastise another
- Exhibiting favouritism, being selective in promotions, favouring members of entourage

- Threatening employees' job security, forcing people to endure hardships
- Ignoring comments, ideas, criticising employees when they speak out, insisting on doing things the old way

Some of the items in the questionnaire of Kathie Pelletier are very illustrative of the nature of mind-sets of 'toxic leaders':

- Inviting a select few to an important meeting.
- Publicly ridiculing an employee's work.
- Mocking employees as a display of humor.
- Yelling when a deadline is missed.
- Threatening to terminate a co-worker, even if the statement is made in a joking manner.

- Asking one of the co-workers, 'Is this the best you can do?'
- Taking credit for an employee's work.
- Inviting specific employees to social events and excluding others.
- Blaming others for the leader's mistakes.

- Ignoring employees' comments.
- Making an employee feel as though his or her job is in jeopardy.
- Lying about the organization's performance at a company meeting.
- Bending the rules to achieve productivity goals.
- Highlighting a work group's achievements in the company newsletter.

- Continuing to do things the old way.
- Making false statements about the competitor.
- Throwing a tantrum when goals are not met.
- Coercing employees to accept his or her ideas.
- Failing to disclose the reasons behind organizational decisions.
- Telling an employee in public that he or she is not a team player.

- Demoting an employee without giving good reason for the decision.
- Telling employees to work and not think.
- Giving resources to departments whose functions make the leader look good.

[Reference: Kathie L. Pelletier, 'Leader toxicity: An empirical investigation of toxic behaviour and rhetoric', Leadership, Vol 6-4, July, 2010]

The Second Orbit of Mental Trap 5:
Self-Doubt and Resource-Myopia

This mental trap is about an inability to decide upon the rudimentary projections of responses-behaviors-actions and dialogues and relationships. It is to be realised that a new idea or a creative and original idea would emerge only faintly.

The 'door' of a new path can ever come only in a tip-of-the-iceberg way. More or less like the poetic inspiration. More or less like the vague imagination about the possibility of some 'force behind the falling of the apple', more or less like the seed of a story or perspective. From this vantage-point, creativity or originality depends significantly on kind of an unconditional trust in the sensitivities and thoughts and feelings – not by any 'knowing'. If 'knowing' and learning was the source of creativity and originality great many more educated brilliant population would have become creative, original, genius individuals.

As most actions are technology driven or automated or comfort-designed, only the designated buttons can be pressed, etc; they indirectly induce self-doubt on the power of the very entity at the non-conscious levels.

The Second Orbit of Mental Trap 6:
Rigidity and Functional Fixedness

Rigidity and functional fixity is expanded and reinforced by the type of work or job of a person. Recall the fact that, every moment the brain is being exercised in its 'doing'. By repeated reciting one learns a poem to be retained forever. If so, repetition of learning and responses-behaviors-actions for decades together must induce rigidity and functional fixedness. It is of some advantage in mechanical activities as that of machine operators. But inappropriate and disadvantageous for managers, leaders, and administrators. Rigidity and functional fixity directly work on affecting the creative and original functions of the engines of intellect [observation, attention, thinking, analysis, conceptualization, etc that are essential for creative ways of managing.

No doubt, repetitive responses-behaviors-actions-dialogues just cannot be avoided in survival-sustenance activities – especially in the modern times. But, if a free-wheeling mind is established, then even the most monotonous work or fixed activity can be done without any element of ennui [boredom of spiralling nature]. For instance, the Rishis could sit at one place for months-years together, lived inside the stony caves for decades, did same rituals and practices, and so on.

Forming of the mental trap of Rigidity and Functional Fixedness
Rigidity helps analysis based on duplicated logics. Helps replication of copied, duplicated, ready-made 'knowings' and 'doings'. Rigidity and functional-fixedness are trained or enforced from early development times. Most of the general mind-sets of 'knowing', 'doing, and 'being' are susceptible to this functional fixity. Obviously, though one cannot know about those that he or she does not know. But, the individual becomes desensitized from the need for variation and looking for alternatives. As a result, he or she tends to continue to respond, behave, act, relate with people, etc in the 'same old ways'.

Development of linkages or causal factors:
1. When several paths of learning were available, you chose the majority one and remained in it, despite your own inner voice contradicting your choice or everyday activities even.
2. You always chose what the social-network colleagues did or according to the majority campaign.
3. You moved around with your mental blocks or traps ever since. When for instance, the others criticized you or commented and made opinions about you, you too became doubtful, 'something wrong with me' kind of internal dialogues begin and frequent inside you [your so-called mind].

The disadvantages of Rigidity:
Rigid or inability to vary the line of thinking, 'knowing', or learning. This helps the parents or peers, teachers or friends to respond, behave, act, talk, and relate easily with children. Rigid self-view, world-views, and others-view. Rigid in responses, behaviors, and actions.

Rigid in the 'doings' of observation, thinking, analysis, conceptualization, dialoguing styles, language usage, rigid in ideologies, attitudes, perspectives, etc.

The expressions of 'rigidity and functional fixity'
Functional-fixedness is reinforced mostly in the ways of 'doing' and in managing one's 'being' - such as ways of eating, sitting, walking, talking, behaving, sleeping, managing the body, mind, etc. But it intervenes in the ways of work: especially teaching, managing people, interacting the same way as usual despite top roles and positions of leadership, etc.

Observe others in the workplace or elsewhere to identify 'rigidity and functional fixity'. That is an effective way to escape your own mental trap of rigidity and functional fixedness. Of course, in a systematised work environment, many or most of the behaviours, actions, dialogues, and relationships may have to rigidly follow certain norms and regulations, procedural requirements. 'Doing' them with absolute tuning is not necessarily rigidity or functional fixity. But, the critical turning point is about the 'awareness' about the ongoing processes. Not as an 'automatic' or "robotic' sort of performance. The trap becomes a critical block only in times of making choices, decisions, and actions.

- Functional-fixedness of language usage - apparent rigidity of the design-setting of physical environment, the ways of interactions with people, etc trains the mindberg to sustain this psychological trap.
- Rigidity in mind-sets and mind-settings: Rigidity in response, behavior, and action, thought, cognition, perception, etc.
- Rigid mind-sets of strictness, severity, and harshness in thoughts,ideas, attitudes, dialogues, etc.
- Strict in opinion, observance, procedure, or method; admitting or allowing of no deviation; scrupulously exact or too precise, unchanging, unvarying; non-adaptive in outlook or responses.
- Rigidity in the 'illusion' of linkage between 'knowing' and 'doing' and 'state-of-being' [that a certain 'knowing' automatically entail the correlated ability in 'doing' or 'states-of-being'.

- 'Articulate Incompetent': Functional-fixedness induced by language - which remains constant and the referents and referent-realities varying.
- Fear of change, fear of discontinuity; Sensitivity-lag.
- Believing that everything or every individual has a specific function within which he or she has to perform.
- Looking at life or work by a formula approach, resisting any changes in approach.
- Uncomfortable with new ideas and new ways of responses, behaviors, and actions trapped thought contents. For example: The caste rigidity and class rigidity in India: for instance, 'I am the Head, I am Senior, I am the Mother, I am an upper caste, etc' kind of 'self-importance'.

This mental trap of rigidity and functional fixity becomes a real block when an individual attempts to try the so-called acts of meditation and yoga, prayers and rituals, dealing with spouse and children; teachers in teaching, and so on.

The Second Orbit of Mental Trap 7:
Lack of Creative Sensitivity or Sensitivity-lag

The sensitivity engines of human beings must be of the highest design. Evidence is the great world of beauty and elegance created by the creative and genius individuals. Ancient *Rishis* of India had the sensitivity to 'see' perhaps the entire realities of Planet Earth and larger universe. Some individuals could sense the past as well as the future.

See the outcomes of creative sensitivity: various forms of art and craft, rhythm and dance, music and painting, etc. All kinds of tools, devices, equipment, systems, engines, machines, etc. Then the infinite range of concepts, ideas, and perspectives. Subject matters of countless types and dimensions. All of them the outputs of the creative sensitivity of a few individuals. Every single item that is used by human beings is a creation of people.

And every trace of creation is possible only by the power of creative sensitivity which is the work of several engines of the intellect in the required sequence and setting.

Creative-sensitivity is likely to be a troublesome concern for the trinity of rulers-clerics-traders. People belonging to one ideology are expected to sustain their centricity-conformity. If the sensitivity of the little child is allowed it will insist the mother to donate anything to a beggar at the gate. If the rich carries any trace of creative sensitivity, then, there cannot be any poverty in the neighbourhoods or in the world itself. Religions are training people to be insensitive to other religions. Innumerable examples may be identified. If you are creatively sensitive.

Leaders of nations are training the citizens to be insensitive to the truth of existence and the universe. Sensitivity-lag or lack of 'creative' sensitivity is quite remarkable in case of critical aspects of existence.

There is the probable lack of 'creative' sensitivity to a majority of population with mental taps:
- body and its processes or 'doings' resulting in various illnesses
- the mind [and its processes] resulting in the lack of self-analysis
- the intelligence resulting in lack of interest in good, higher, and great knowledge
- the attendant-spirit [the core inside, or self, or psyche, soul, 'atman' or the linkages with metaphysical realities, etc] resulting in severe identity crisis.

Body: Every cat and dog knows its body states and manage it in good Tao ['tuning with integrity', in 'good flow'] evidenced by lack of fatigue or weaknesses of any sort, low rate of illnesses, avoid climatic variations that may affect them, what to eat how much to eat, when to sleep, etc] - complete alertness always. Such sensitivity is miserably lacking in human beings. In the beginning, every child knows when to eat, how much to eat, and even what to eat. But that is corrupted by the centricity-conformity with the mechanical knowledge of the parents, peers, teachers, guides, popular literature, etc.

Mind: Except a handful, the majority of the interviewed sample of at least 15,00+ individuals had no idea about their own minds. They were completely ignorant about the fact that their observations, perceptions, thinking, etc are driven by the non-conscious part of the mindberg. Very few believed that there is a real unconscious side for the mind which determines their expressions, responses, actions, relationships, dialogues, etc. Nobody knew that the unconscious is the dominant part of the mind. Because of the lack of creative sensitivity to one's own mindberg, the populations find it difficult to control the damaging emotions and feelings, thoughts and aspirations, and so on.

Attendant Spirit: There must be an 'energy field' or spirit attendant or present in the body other than all the anatomical physiological details. Needless to say, without creative sensitivity, that 'spirit' cannot be touched. The so-called realization-of-self, or enlightenment, or Satori is simply impossible without driving the engines of creative sensitivity.

Significance of Creative-Sensitivity:
Sensitivity or 'creative sensitivity' is the real gate to creativity, originality, and genius. The 'sensitivity' referred-to here is located in the original free-floating functions of the intellect engines - often manifested by every child.

Question:
Why sensitivity is not triggered to its natural entelechy of touching the 'attendant spirit or genius state-of-being?
Answer:
Because of the 'sensitivity-lag' of parents, teachers, guides. The process of inducting a child into the world of adults is based on the analysis of life-work-relationships, wrong 'attributions' of causality, conformity-centricity driven ideas by the mental traps of parents, peers, teachers, guides, etc. Due to ordinary or mediocre interactions with the child, the 'sensitivities' probable-possible for the original-mind remain dormant, the development environment even 'prevented' the 'original search response' of the engines-of-intellect, spirit, that appear or manifest invariably in a child.

For the majority of children - even external senses and their sensitivities are not exposed to various kinds of aesthetics of existence. Of course, children are exposed to whatever the parents and guides and teachers are interested in. Most of them carry mental traps of medium to high levels.

Parents consider children 'enjoying' their 'pleasure principle'. But seldom take them to higher sensitivities – such as to classical arts, music, dance, theatre, craft, good reading, etc; to varied cultures, practices, types of events and people, unique spaces and locations, etc. The development environment almost prevents or blocks the nature-process-provided engines that work behind 'creative sensitivity' [the higher 'cortical functions of the brain': the ultimate or the only uniqueness of human species: music, dance, art, poetry, appreciation and wonder about entities, things, and phenomena, aesthetics-of-existence, etc].

The Disadvantages of Sensitivity Lag
To repeat, 'sensitivity' is the greatest power of the engines-of-intellect. Creativity, originality, and especially genius is possible only by sensitivity. To repeat: all art, poetry, literature, painting, music, theatre, film, fiction; sciences, technologies, philosophies, and so on are primarily the outcomes of the 'creative sensitivities' of a few individuals.

Due to 'Sensitivity Lag':
- Low or no sensitivity to the deeper dimensions of life-work and relationships, entities, things, and phenomena, people, and self one's own.
- Poor attention to details resulting in the disuse of original sensitivities of the entity to signals, cues, clues of all kinds… especially, blind to the more critical linkages of the 'invisible-hidden-subtle orbits of referent-realities [in the context and-or requirements].
- Poor observation, reflection, conceptualization, etc.
- No extra abilities of performing arts, literature, reading, etc.
- Low imagination, visualization, creative dialoguing, etc.
  [This kind of 'low-ness' in genius is not a matter of inferiority for the great majority of educated population..!]

- Missing the romantic, softer, aesthetic value or attitude to sexuality; instead, it is driven by the physical and unrefined perspectives duplicated from clandestine sources.

Without creative sensitivities, life-work-relationships become peripheral: 'living by bread alone' level of existence. The climate and culture of families, institutions, organizations become insipid and mechanical; relationship of spouses become un-romanitc and dull and routine-based.

The rote-learning based education suppresses individual sensitivities to aspects of the details of the world. The so-called Management education is nothing but inducing mechanical 'knowing' in certain exclusive subject domains. It 'trains' the mind, intellect, and spirit to contract the Newtonian mechanical self-view and world-view. In other words, a person with super sensitivity to a technology domain tends to be insensitive to the poverty in the very neighbourhood. The leaders become insensitive to the tragedies of citizens. The managers and leaders did not seem to be sensitive to domains of philosophies, denied appreciation of the so-called occult subjects [which are placed in the 'low-class' category].

The highly 'ideologically-sensitive' political, religious, administration leaders are not equally sensitive to the problems of the low caste, poorest of poor, nomadic homeless legions of people. Nations keep aside their true sensitivities about the conditions of other nations. And so on. The entire human existence is made great by the sensitivities of creative and original and genius individuals. And some of the leaders are mismanaging and mutilating life – using those very knowings and doings of technologies.

Most business corporations do not follow ethical practices and sustain their sheer primitive 'trade mentality' and manipulation of their so-called customers and the relevant populations. In India, as of now, the great part of wealth and richness of the whole land is under the custody and control of just one-percent of the population. Same is the situation in the statistical world. The rich and powerful are conveniently insensitive to the realities of the populations and societies.

Their minds and intellects are terribly trapped in sensitivity-lag. Meanwhile, the majority is contented in their mental traps backed up by ego defense mechanisms. The statistical findings and media reports provide ample evidences. The details of life of populations are damaged by mental traps.

The Second Orbit of Mental Trap 8: The Familiarity-Trap Contempt | Taken-for-Granted Attitude Towards the Familiar

Familiarity Trap is not a part of the PNK-Questionnaire.
But such a mind-set has been identified during the hundreds of training programs occurred in the context of mental traps. Actually, anyone can discern such a trap in oneself as well as in others, in the very functions of the engines of social processes and administration and governments.

Familiarity-Trap works in tricky ways. One way: the familiar things are taken for granted and-or treated with contempt. The other way, yet, the person tends to do things only in the familiar way. No new or suggested variation or change is accepted or tolerated. Unfamiliar things are not noticed. In the noticed things, only the familiar items are chosen for consideration.

The Way of Familiarity Trap
First of all, the Familiarity trap drives a 'taken-for-granted' attitude or even contempt towards things, events, people, ideas, entities, and even one's own self and life. External and internal expressions of 'contempt', added. A fresh entrant into a job, any job, is very careful, concerned, dedicated etc to the work for the first few weeks or months and gradually become a victim of familiarity trap and may take the details for granted. Reportedly, the life of modern couples end up in boredom and dullness within a few years. The plenty of interactions with people around makes the marital companionship an aspect of taken for granted attitude. Such an attitude is clearly conveyed in the proverb: "The Jasmine in the courtyard is of no fragrance". The Jasmine in one's own courtyard is 'taken-for-granted' because it is all the time there. There is no mind-set to go to it, touch and feel its leaves, smell a flower, and so on.

As a phrase 'taken-for-granted' refers to the following:

- fail to appreciate someone or something that is very familiar or obvious [for example: 'the comforts that people take for granted' | '..she took him for granted']
- take something for granted; assuming that something is true without questioning it or self-verifying it.

Keyword 1: Familiarity

- close acquaintance with or knowledge of something
- the quality of being well known; recognizability based on long or close association
- relaxed friendliness or intimacy between people
- inappropriate and often offensive informality of behavior or language
- **Proverb: "Familiarity breeds contempt":** extensive use or interaction or close association with someone or something, idea or event, etc leading to a loss of respect for it.

Keyword 2: 'Contempt'

- the feeling that a person or a thing is beneath consideration, worthless, or deserving scorn
- disregard for something that should be taken into account
- [also contempt of court] the offense of being disobedient to or disrespectful of a court of law and its officers
- to consider someone or something to be unworthy of respect or attention
- the feeling that a person or a thing or an event is beneath consideration, worthless, or deserving scorn.

The familiarity trap is evidenced in:

- The expressions, responses, behaviours, actions, work, relationships of Centricity-Conformity + Rigidity and Functional Fixedness + Sensitivity-Lag.
- Manifested in the 'taken-for-granted' attitude to people, events, entities, ideas, things, phenomena and one's own responses, behaviors, and actions and self-life-work and relationships.

- Manifested in the relative inability to appreciate the 'already available' in the environment and in one's own life-work and relationships.
- In the inability to see, experience, feel the wonder and beauty of the available facilities [wherever] and crave, desire, aspire for the 'next' best – things, facilities, positions, possessions, etc. Feeling bored, dissatisfied, disillusioned about life and self etc. For instance, there would be mind-sets about genius, creativeness, spirituality etc in almost everyone – but are 'taken-for-granted'.
- By the familiarity trap, people develop presumptions and stereotypes and biases; fail to observe the limits of what is permitted or appropriate;develop attitudes of impudence, impertinence, disrespect and even open expressions of contempt for certain 'type' of ideas, events, situations or certain category of people, entities, and phenomena.
- By the familiarity trap 'nothing is satisfying'...
- **Only the tips are noticed - the icebergs are taken-for-granted**

BY the familiarity trap, there can be frequent conflicts in nuclear families. Seemingly, taken-for-granted are the guidelines provided in the classic religious treatises such as Gita, Bible, etc; messages of the mystics and rishis; supreme guidelines and perspectives on existence - such as 'Ahimsa', 'Man is made in the form of the God', 'Satyam Eva Jayate', and so on. The declarations of the great geniuses of India such as Vivekananada, J Krishnamurthy, Tagore, and so on are taken-for-granted.

Even deities and their ideas are closed in the familiarity trap.
The so-called 'low' castes and communities, and minority-remote classes of people are taken for granted and marginalised. If you reflect for a minute about the implications of whatever presented above, you will realize aspects in your life, work, relationships that are taken-for-granted or treated with contempt.

If familiar things are taken-for-granted, what is that single thing which is inevitably the most familiar for anyone?

The vicious-circle of 'taken-for-granted' attitude in India:
Familiarity trap could very well be a global phenomena, but its scope and extent is likely to be extremely high in India as evidenced in the case division-separation, and other religious-political-education phenomena.

Finally, individuals seem to be taking their own selves for granted because of the Familiarity Trap. Even the proudest arrogant looking person too has actually taken himself for granted. The body, mind, intelligence, intellect, and spirit, prayers, and deities, are seemingly taken for granted. Perhaps, due to the lack of sensitivity to do any firm-elegant-taoic-correct-and-complete examination and verification. The quality of expressions, responses, behaviours, actions, and dialogues is affected by Familiarity-Trap. Relationships are under Familiarity-Trap: 'matha-pitha-gurus', spouses and children and siblings; neighbourhoods and ecology; and what not.

Above all, the work, role functions, responsibilities, power and authority are taken under familiarity trap. Expert drivers make accidents. Pedestrians, cleanliness, civic duties are dealt with contempt, disregard and abandonment.

The food is taken-for-granted, language is taken-for-granted, human beings are taken-for-granted, education, planet earth, and even the so-called God is taken-for-granted. Road accidents, or accidents in workplaces, perhaps, all kinds of accidents are due to the taken-for-granted attitude.

The miserable lack of quality and completeness in learning and doing is observable in the bureaucracy of India; unethical activities of the business and trade owners, product pricing, favouritism of power holders, food adulteration, bribery, nepotism, all kinds of corruption, various direct and indirect ways of political manipulations taking the voting populations for granted, etc. Some of the nation leaders are masters in taken-for-granted attitude towards humanity itself. Annihilation of masses, misuse of ecosystems and nature resources, and so on... Examples aplenty.

The Familiarity Trap and creativity, originality, genius...

As mentioned before, perhaps, the most taken-for-granted aspect is one's own self; its true and correct and elegant completeness is never searched. Truth in the external world is insisted and fought for, the truth of one's own life is not a concern. Existence is under familiarity trap, along with the planet Earth. The value of one's work and relationships and existence is perhaps discerned by the end of the journey. Seldom came across an retired person who had the firm confidence about the completeness and quality of his or her work-life. Students take their studies for granted. Perhaps schools and teachers do the same with their work, their students, as well as their subject matters. 'Karmanyeva adhikarasthe, ma phaleshu kadacana' is taken for granted, in the very land where the deity of that idea is glorified. The ancient Indian original ideas, methods of education, and perspectives too are under familiarity trap.

All creations, discoveries, inventions, innovations, modifications; poetry, art, literature, music, dance, theatre, craft, and so on are inspired by familiar and familiar items only. That were all taken-for-granted by the others. Your entity, any part of it will never talk to you or draw your attention and inform you that 'please do this, please develop that', and so on. The total potentiality, or the entelechies of the entity are not on display anywhere inside you, in such a way that you simply choose one-or-more of them and develop them. In fact, the probable-possible entelechies of the human entities are manifested in the varied activities of many individuals - labelled genius, mystic, original, inventive, etc; supreme artists in various fields, etc. Or even the great glorified deities who declared: 'Thou art that'.

If you take the great acts and performances in all the range of human activities, every one of them is an example of human entelechies. When you see someone performing music, then it is a signal for you to verify whether you also have that potential or not. When someone dances, writes poetry, does painting, or magic, or play games and gymnastics, achieves scholastic heights; manifests mystic and spiritual evolution - it is to be taken as an evidence to realize that such and such are the engine-powers provided to the human entity as a common entelechy.

Not as an exclusive power, specially god-given power ONLY to a few individuals.When someone does any act with firm-correct-elegant-taoic completeness, whether it is cooking or writing or calligraphy, or in the way of responses, behaviors, and dialogues you become impressed.
In other words, why not try your possibilities – having all those marvellous engines, god-given engines?

So, not testing, not verifying, not developing any of the entelechies of the human entity that is with you IS the clear evidence of the familiarity trap. Let it be so with the great majority. Of course, it is a matter of choice, decision, and action of trap-free minds. By consciously choosing and doing them the mental traps may vanish also.

As a paradox of all mental traps, you never take you for granted.
You live completely to do whatever you are familiar within you. For instance, you learned some subject-matters, got through the interview, do your job, work for promotion and develop a career, got married, save money, get a house, buy vehicles and electronics and good dresses, seek social-networking, and remain in the good books of relevant people and friends, etc. Yes, you do the best and never take you for granted. You are again tricked into familiarity trap only. You cannot go beyond whatever is familiar to you within you. And you think that whatever familiar to you comprises the only possibility.

Familiarity Trap and Genius
Unlike creativity and originality which depends upon external factors and facilities, genius is the birthright of every individual. The term genius is highly misunderstood by the great majority. Their perceptions about genius is based on centricity and conformity to the media images and stories about genius individuals - not the phenomenon of genius.

The English term genius means: The attendant Spirit of a person. There are other meanings given in the dictionaries. They are added in order to rationalize the majority mind-set perception of genius 'individuals' - not the way genius exists as reality of the phenomenon in every human being.

It is the genius in you to choose the primary root meaning.
Genius in Sanskrit equivalent is 'nisarga' which means 'swa-bhava-nirmoksha'. That is, to render freedom ['nirmoksha'] to the 'bhavas' [or expressions, responses, capabilities and entelechies] of the 'swa' - one's own original self. But the original self is taken-for-granted and a duplicated set of knowings is established as the self. Perhaps, the most familiar aspect in the world for an individual is his or her own 'swa' - present every moment, throughout day and night and till the end. The most familiar 'swa' one's own is quite vulnerable to be taken-for-granted.

The way to search genius inside is by working upon the intellect engines. NOT by chasing it by the meanings and media reports about it.

Inside the Familiarity Trap: The 'taken-for-granted attitude'
The body, intelligence, mind, intellect, and spirit
Obviously, mindberg is nothing but mind-sets and one is living with those mind-sets that are formed during non-conscious times. Non-conscious in the sense that primary orbit of mind-sets driven by the invariant of anxiety-fear-displeasure are all in the non-conscious realms of the mindberg. As one is always with his or her mindberg, it IS the very self [person is for the observers, there is no 'separate person' for a person..!]. Then its ways of functions cannot be discerned. But its manifestations such as fear, conflict, etc are 'sensed'. The manifestations of the mindberg becomes the very self. And the mind-sets drive the manifestations of external responses, behaviors, and actions as well as internal experience.

The Second Orbit of Mental Trap 9:
Self-Importance and Speed
Self-Importance is entirely different from Self-Respect

The concept-sense of 'self-importance':
'Full of one's own importance' is well known phrase in English language. It denotes 'having a very high opinion of oneself'. That, it is an English phrase itself is the evidence that this mental trap is rather universal.

It is a naturally possible-probable outcome of human learning and development. The parents, teachers, guides, peers, relatives, etc would nevertheless contribute to the development of 'self-importance' in the child. When they intimidate, restrict, block, rebuke, prevent, etc they consciously induce the mind-set of self-importance also. Possibly, the other mental traps are enforced on behalf of that climax state of 'self-importance'. It is because of the importance given to the child that some other mental traps are induced.

For instances:
Why the child is restricted from facing ambiguities and uncertainties, strange and new things and people, etc?

- It is to establish the self-importance that the child is trained to belong to certain special as well as specific conformities and centricities.
- It is to sustain the 'successes' of the important child that failure should be avoided at any cost.
- It is to nurture and sustain the importance of self that the child shall not do anything that invites criticisms, and blames, and critical reviews.
- It is to maintain the status quo that the child is desensitized from the problems and troubles of life, other citizens, and humanity in general.

Every child is playful and highly sensitive to entities, things, phenomena in the nature-process. But the parents-teachers-guides ensure that such sensitivities are considered a waste of time and initiative. Of course, unless such activities can contribute to self-importance. Parents try their best contribution to ensure high academic performance. Extra-curricular activities are supported only if they can lead to recognition or awards and self-importance thereof.

Self-Importance is based on 'Knowings'. Not on 'Doing' or 'Being'
Knowings about one's background, education, social status, richness, role positions, fame, popularity, public acceptance, recognition, and so on. It is based on 'I think, therefore, I am'. Not I experience, therefore, I am.

None of the class-caste-richness; fame-wealth or number-1-ness in the world, local or larger world, kind of 'importance' in the world and so on get inside the 'body' of the individual. Never as a direct sensing or feeling or experience. Nor into the engines of intellect or attendant spirit. Nor into the 'being'. In fact, self-importance could be the final great block to Satori or enlightenment.

In reality, for those who have the tuning with the being, this fact can be clearly known also. That is, if there is tuning with the 'being', none of the fame or richness or number-1 position makes any difference at all. However, some one else's richness, fame, popularity, power, importance etc are 'felt' by the audience and audience only. Because of their fear and anxiety about 'lowness' and 'humiliation' perceived out of the relative lack of those decorations.

Speed Trap: A trap of the current times

The 'Speed Mind-set' that drives 'a state of hurried and impatient ways of responses, behaviors, and actions and dialogues; managing work and relationships'. The will and patience essential to read great books, the inspiration to master new activities, such as games, crafts, arts, or musical instruments, etc of children are absolutely corrupted by the speed trap - of course, mainly induced by the internet, smart phones, high-speed vehicles, etc. By the speed-trap of the parents and teachers as well.

By the 'speed-trap' there could be needless anxiety and panic about simple and silly actions and perception and analysis of requirements. The mind-intellect-spirit cannot sense, feel, appreciate and enjoy the wonder of life, of the simple things in life, of the small-and-beautiful, relationships, romantic relationships with people and nature, with plants and birds and rivers, etc.

Even normal attention to children, colleagues, friends, people, events, things, etc in the surroundings get contaminated by speed. It corrupts mind-sets of patience and gratitude, inducing inner chaos in 'waiting'; 'tensions' of various kinds in finishing the work inducing the so-called work-pressure, etc.

113

The speed-trap blocks the learning activity by impatience - often manifested by poor performers. It also blocks mastery over any 'doing'. And much more.

Speed is good. There is a certain natural speed of growth of body, of thinking, of respiration, heartbeat, talking, eating, writing, etc [there is 'range' and optimum speed for everything - such as the speed of the revolution and rotation of planet Earth]. But an obsession with speed can be a trap, that it dilutes learning, drives the compulsion to seek and use 'techniques', short cuts for things – unethical practices, craving for quick results; impatience and tension about finishing one's own work as well as others' work, and so on. Gradually, the energy-fields of the mindberg become set to speed; unable to achieve the calmness of the natural speed. No activities is done with the required care and dedication; including sexuality and worship.

Of course, the mind is always in a threshold speed. But if that speed is increased it will drag irrelevant and inappropriate mind-sets into motion. People want quick results, quick returns, quick progress, to become number one as fast as possible, etc. The entrepreneurs and business houses are doing haywire because of the speed trap to achieve more profits and increase in their size and operations. By the speed trap, internet sources are quickly referred to instead of gathering complete knowledge. No reading of great books because of speed traps only. Management students are craving for 'techniques' than mastering methods. By the forward jumps of speed-trap, whatever gathered as wealth and money and possessions do not satisfy people. One possession and its happiness to be soon replaced with the need for another speed. The worshippers and disciples want quick results, direct meeting with the very super God as quickly as possible.

See the linkages of speed trap with creativity and originality.
Perhaps the number one requirement of a creative, or original, or genius individual is the freedom from speed trap. The mindberg is very likely to get inspiring perceptions, feelings, and intuitions; the intellect might be capable of conceptualizing, attention, visualization, and so on. But speed corrupts them. The 'speed mind-set' camouflages the inspiration and will to work. One may end up insulting and humiliating one's own body, mind, intellect, and spirit.

The main blocking aspects of the 'speed trap' are:
- corrupting the mind-sets of patience and perseverance,
- retarding the engine power of the will and mind-set for 'hard-work and repeated practicing',
- 'no-mood' or boredom for re-working, trying variations of a work, etc.

Now technologies have enabled super-speed to many of the regular activities of survival-sustenance, work, and ways of relating with people. High speed vehicles, high speed travel by which great number of people move from one location to other. Electronic mail, internet, and so on. But, to what extent all these 'speeds' have contributed to anything fundamental to the life of people remains to be dubious. Poverty, global and local, is equally speeding up to cover more and more locations and populations.

And, of course, entire design-setting-process of almost all activities of businesses are done in higher and higher speeds due to technologies of various planes. The market is flooded with high speed supply of all possible-probable products. If this speed continues, there is the scope for a major break down. Or some sort of accidents. You may identify the nature of 'speed-trap' that are manifested everywhere around you, at home, neighbourhood, on the road, in the workplace, in the local and larger surroundings, etc.

The reality of existence, all nature processes, is in a 'present continuous tense'. The so-called God must be in the present continuity. Neither in the unknown deep past at the moment of creation [if at all] or waiting to appear in any future. The world of our perimeters has reached only till the present split-second. So life-work-relationships are to managed in their proper speeds. Greedy needs, motives, goals and desires place an obsession with speed. Quick results: one side. The craving to prolong life as much as to immortality: the other side. It may not be easy to differentiate the ways in which speed-trap operates in the current setting and processes of survival-sustenance. Because, almost 97 percent of educated-intelligent populations carry minimum 2-3 mental traps. Their ways of behaviours, expressions, actions, responses, dialogues, work, and relationships are defined by that trap in the non-conscious. Permeating every aspect of life. In seeking need-gratification, from basic drives to self-realization. Including in man-woman relationships, especially in the context of sexuality.

The third orbit of consequences of mental traps

A thing cannot identify itself. It requires something else.
In order to detect the presence of mental traps in the behaviours and actions of others, it requires clarity about them. Even if a mental rap is identified, it is not easy to explain and provide clear evidences. If done carelessly, the others may not agree or may become hostile.

From the vantage-point of mental traps:
Life is a tale of sound and fury signifying the role of mental traps.

The details of consequences depend upon the nature of the self, level of life, work, education, experience, relationships, location, etc of an individual. However, certain general consequences may be differentiated. The mental traps work behind almost every expression, response, behaviour, action, work, relationship of the usual normal distribution minds or statistical minds of at least 70 per cent of the educated and employed populations in India.

It must be repeated that, threshold level mental-'blocks' are an inevitable and clearly essential requirement for survival-sustenance and adaptation with the social setting and people. However, mental traps becomes a real block to achieve existential purposes – as they trap the individual from moving out of the given 'box' of expressions, responses, behaviours, actions, work, relationships; thoughts and dialogues.

The mental traps are manifested not only at the level of individuals but also of groups, institutions, organizations, nations, and governments. Mental traps define the relations between nations or in the stances adopted by the leaders of the nations. As the parents and others carry mental traps, children are trained or forced and guided to imitate, duplicate, and adopt responses, behaviors, and actions that are comfortable and convenient for them. The extent and type of that convenience is determined by the extent and type of mental traps of the parents. Children of divorced parents may become victims of the mental traps in a medium to high degree, needlessly.

116

Mental traps delimit the level and quality of 'knowing'

The 9 mental 'traps' block or delimit the original powers of the engines of mind, intellect, and spirit. The mental traps sort of betray the self of a person. They delimit the firm, correct, completeness of a 'knowing'.

The three core components of a human being are 'knowing', 'doing' and 'being'. Yet, 'knowing' is the core. Because, it is a man-created world. The new entrant must have to 'learn' or 'know' everything including how to eat. The 'doing' and the 'being' are subjects of 'knowing'. Even the core, the 'self' also is to be known. Everything of the 'knowing' 'doing' and 'state-of-being' is linkaged with the self – the I, me, my [that 'sensation' of self within - the operating entity]. The personal history of a human being, whatsoever in the given time-space-location. The 'self-image' is very critical. And that self image includes the basic grounding of mental traps.

Because of the mental trap linkages with 'knowing', interaction with individuals having unique specialities, and greater levels of knowledge, etc may be curtailed. Instead, such entities are glorified or deified and declare as separate kind of human beings so that the populations can continue in the deep slumber inside the comfort zones of their mental traps.

Racial struggles and killings, hatred and jealousy and war, etc are due to mental traps about knowing. They are due to certain traps of 'knowing'. Mental traps induce conflicts between spouses, among relatives and friends, between groups and associations, political and religious ideology subscribers, or between nations. Quite logically, mental traps are the cause of all mental problems, disorders of behaviours, and anomalies in relationships.

The mental traps tend to sustain prejudices, narrow-minded parochialism; trigger biases, dislike, hostility, and related unjust and unethical behaviors and actions. Using the mental traps of rigidities and sensitivity-lags populations are persuaded, forced and-or directed-guided to belong to groups or ideologies disregarding and disrespecting their true identities.

Protagonists of pure sciences look at art, humanities, and philosophies with ridicule or disdain. Humanity is divided-separated NOT by ideologies and vantage-points, or religions. But by the mental traps linkaged with them. What else?

Mental traps affect the elegance and completeness of 'doing'

At a primary level, mental traps reduce the quality or firm, correct, elegant, completeness of 'doing'. The 'cat-ness' or genius of the human entity is blocked.

The process of 'knowing' can be done without the intervention of mental traps. But not the 'doings'. There are no tests and examinations about knowing in ideologies of ethics, religion, civics, or about beliefs, values, attitudes, and so on. But, in the 'doing' of those 'knowings' – there is the scope for block by the mental traps, and they become 'tested' in work, life, relationship settings.

The mental traps that block the quality of 'doing', learning of new activities, managing unfamiliar activities, etc are more powerful and deep rooted than the mental traps to 'knowing'. Because of mental traps the learners are not able to translate their 'knowing' into 'doing'.

The mental traps suppress 'doings' based on even genuine inspirations, desires, and purposes in life. Three or more mental traps intervene the learning or 'doing' of attempting a new thing: fear-anxiety-tension about [1] ambiguous or strange; as a new thing or action is liable to be ambiguous, [2] failure; as the new action may invite failure or errors, [3] humiliation; as some observers may pose criticism, [4] centricity and conformity; as for example, if someone decides to learn a new musical instrument or start reading books at home the spouse or visitors may make unwarranted comments, and so on.

Every individual self is sort of a manager or leader or driver of the great corporation of a human entity. When every bird and cat is complete in its responses, behaviours, and actions, the human beings are much slow and below the threshold levels of entelechies.

The engines-of-entity are ever ready to be trained or to be shaped to do the 'doing' of anything originally probable-possible for it. All that great range of human activities and performances are the evidence. The entity carries the potentialities to enjoy music, rhythm, dance, colour and design variations, events-entities-phenomena that are beautiful and wonderful, and so on.

See: 'doing' is the core. All outcomes are by 'doing': orgasm, quenching of thirst and hunger, finding spaces of safety-security, discovering belongingness and love, identifying ways of self-esteem, and finally the enlightenment or Satori.

In other words, the human creature is capable and ready to sing, dance, paint, and it has the great engines-of-intellect of attention, reflection, cognition and perception, thinking, analysis, imagination, intuition, visualization, dreaming, etc, But the mindberg is strapped. Its original free-wheeling is blocked by certain trained, duplicated, imposed mind-sets, called mental traps.

Mental traps may disrupt or reduce the speeds and powers of the intellect-engines of observation, attention, reflection, thinking, cognition, perception, intuition, imagination, visualization, analytic conceptualization, and so on. Thereby, the possible-probable creative, original, and genius levels - present in at least thirty percent of human entities - are restricted and blocked.

So if the creature-entity is allowed to go through [practice..!] the details of an activity, it will do the learning and mastery of it. But the person's mind needs the required creative sensitivities.

Mental traps and the 'state-of-Being': Identity Crisis
Mental traps reduce clarity about the identity, self-image, self-description, perspective or purpose in life-work-relationships. A mind-setting of high mental traps can disrupt the integrity of character and reduce self-respect. [See the identity crisis of the 'cook' in the Zen parable given elsewhere in the book].

For instance, high degree of fear-tension-anxiety of failure or of humiliation may drive some people to try unethical means of gathering power and wealth. A group that originally plans the criminal manipulations can easily trap people with undefined or unclear identities. It is a paradox that, on one side there is the mental trap of fear-tension-anxiety about ambiguity and uncertainty. But on the other side, the very self-image and identity is ambiguous and uncertain.

The self and self-image are different. For instance, a person actually may carry a self of high positive qualities but may 'under-estimate' on the basis of the mental traps.

The mental traps tend to sustain prejudices, biases, dislike, hostility, and related unjust behaviours and actions. Using the mental traps of rigidities and sensitivity-lags people may be directed to belong to groups or ideologies disregarding and disrespecting the views and ideologies of the 'others'.

Certain 'ideas' when linkaged with mind-sets of mental traps trigger wars and conflicts as groups disregard or disrespect ideologies of the 'others' just because they represent different vantage-points. Protagonists of pure sciences look at art, humanities, and philosophies with disregard or disdain. Humanity is divided by mental traps linkaged to ideologies and vantage-points of religions.

Mental traps delimit the 'flow' of the spirit of the human entity
First of all, the entelechies of the entity are not fulfilled. The real probable-possible scope or purpose of existence [of the entity] becomes delimited by the missing freedom of the mind and intellect.

Second of all, the evolution of consciousness to that of a self-realized, self-actualized individual; a genius individual, or a creative-original individual, or a happy-contented individual, etc is thwarted. Mental traps prevent achieving tuning with the super-consciousness [that covers the totality of the entity and all its manifestations].

Instead, the consciousness becomes delimited to the normal awareness about ongoing life, personal history, various mind-sets of worries and pains, losses, and so on usually sensed by anyone.

By all existent theories and observations, the human entities carry tendencies or motivations of a hierarchical order. From the basic needs of food, sexuality, safety, security, love, belongingness; then the 'higher-needs' of self esteem, achievement, power, actualization, etc. The 'needs' can be formed in the mindberg as a result of spontaneous processes of growth-and-development or by duplication and imitation, or by compulsions of others, or by sheer centricity-conformity. For instance, anyone can desire for top rank in university examinations. But it requires certain abilities; the will, patience, hard work, etc.

Someone may have the will and patience but may not have the abilities required to do a certain program. In other words, there is a real requirement of potentialities to achieve the needed state or wanted positions. The little child has to develop control over hand movements in order to fulfill the need of writing something. Same is the case with the higher order needs. One just cannot hope for self-esteem without the required powers and potentialities, mind-sets and perspectives. One cannot aspire for enlightenment without the required engine powers. Now, one or more of the mental traps block the development of the engine powers or potentialities. As a result, the real probable-possible entelechy of the entity is prevented. [Entelechy: a single word that refers to: identifying + real-izing or actual-izing the potentialities].

Third of all, the mental traps prevent the opening of greater 'states-of-being'. The mental traps prevent the 'nir-moksha' of the 'bhavas' of the 'swa' [**'sarga'** - the Sanskrit equivalent of genius means: 'swa-bhava-nir-moksha']. The entity senses great lot of signals but they are not noticed and reflected upon by the mind ['mindberg is the person': 'I mind, therefore also, I am']. For instance, the entity or creature feels good about eating when hungry. And if someone offers food, the entity would feel great sense of happiness and gratitude – somewhat like a dog often manifests. But the mindberg does not consider it.

So, when you feed someone in need of food, his or her creature-entity feels good about it. There is an energy transaction – even though the recipient may not show or say anything in return. Similarly, if you injure, humiliate, intimidate someone to the effect of damaging the entity, there could be correlated 'returns'.

Fourth of all, the mental traps intervene and affect the quality of the 'mental economy*'. In reality, all the environment settings of systems, procedures, processes, rules, norms, governance, products and services of immense range, etc are designed and set for improving the 'process quality of life'. From that quality, a better state of mind or peace or happiness. A great 'mental economy'. All so-called progress, scientific and technologic advantages, advancement in economic, social, political situations; etc are for facilitating ever better living conditions for maximum number of people.

But, despite all such evolutions and actualizations in the external world of life, work, and social interfaces, the quality of 'mental economy' are deteriorated. Increase in the number of mind-sets that are linkaged with mental blocks and traps and defenses is the core reason. Such expansion of the 'base mind-sets' of a mental trap would gradually corrode the will-to-live or corrupt the purpose of life or meaning in life. Sensitivity lag would reduce the respect and wonder about life, demean values and principles, introduce doubt and hatred, animosity and aggression. Several such mind-sets would germinate out of the interaction of such mental traps.

Increasing dependence on the virtual world delimits direct interface with events, people, and signals, things, events, entities, and phenomena in Nature. [Human beings are primarily only 'creatures' of this planet Earth - like any bird or cat]. The various original engines of the human entity become disused and atrophied by the continuity of mental traps. Already the number of young people who behave, respond, act, and talk like zombies is increasing. It will turn to a critical mass within a maximum of about two decades. The extent and pattern of blocking mind-sets accelerate the process of becoming a 'zombie'.*

*Zombie: a person who is or appears lifeless, apathetic, or completely
     unresponsive to his or her surroundings.

Note on the concept of 'Mental Economy'
The concept refers to 'the state of mind derived out of the feedback
perception or others' feedback about the nature and quality of
responses, behaviours, actions, work, manifested or expressed and
their consequences in self, life, and relationships of the individual'.

The mental traps vis-à-vis hierarchy of work-life responsibilities

When the hierarchy or network of responsibility increases the function
of mental traps become evident. In normal usual responses-behaviors-
actions-dialogues everything is within the comfort zone of mental traps.
To talk in groups no mental traps. But to talk to an audience? To sing
in the bathroom no mental traps. But to sing in a public competition?
Almost any 'knowing' is free from traps, unlike most of the 'doings'.

Mental traps and 'depression': All worries and problems, confusions
and conflicts, depressions and disappointments, etc are due to mental
traps only. Self-humiliation versus self-importance, sensitivity-lag versus
the VUCA world, self-doubt versus requirement of action together tend
to induce the so-called 'depression', identity crisis, and various internal
struggles. Then individual may try to adjust these anomalies by drugs and
alcohol, excessive eating, violent language wherever possible, etc.
If none of these works, then there is ennui or deadly boredom tending
towards suicidal thoughts, severe sense of meaninglessness and
emptiness, restlessness, insomnia, psychosomatic illnesses,
and individual specific anomalies, etc.

Mental traps corrupt 'self-perception' [cognition and perception of self
and responses, behaviors, actions, and dialogues thereof; like the world
is perceived non-consciously and sometimes consciously, the self too is
perceived].

Self means, whatever that you are aware of as the 'you' or the 'I'. The 'that' which is in charge of doing this reading right now. The that which does the 'doings' of dialogues, responses, behaviors, actions, and dialogues. The that which lives the life-work-relationships. One can sense or verify his or her 'self', by being alert to the stream-of-consciousness, or whatever thoughts that suggested an activity when you are alone for some time. That self is the operator functioning in the survival and sustenance plane, 'knowing' of things, 'doing' of things, and relating with people and signals, things, events, entities, and phenomena.

But, children are not trained for self-perception and self-analysis. The child is never asked to 'think' about himself or herself. The students are never asked to 'think' or to 'reflect'. The school system is totally oblivious to the reality of 'intellect' which generated all 'intelligences' [knowledge of all possible range].

Often, the others around give feedback that reinforce the mental traps. When asked for self-description [done at least for 60-70 percent of trainees], almost 95 percent could provide only a report of their bio-data. Trapped in the bio-data but not about any great self-perception or self-image. Not in the 'genius' within.

What could be the probable-possible self-perception of a creative, original, genius individual? A mystic leader? If he is asked to reflect upon his self, what would be the contents of his responses or descriptions? And what will be yours? In fact, most theories of creativity and genius got trapped in whatever the samples of creative and genius individuals described about themselves and their 'acts of creation'.

The meaning and implications of the term 'genius' got 'corrupted' because of the descriptions created by writers, biographers, researchers, and media about genius individuals. The 'sample' provided superlative dialogues and descriptions about their 'linkage perceptions'. Therefore, the term genius is defined in the dictionaries [as one with extraordinary intellect', 'specially gifted' and so on as if the creating aspect or god is a political entity that selected some human entities to be extraordinary].

The original term genius referred to: 'the attendant spirit of a person' - reported at several places in the book to reinforce it or to have the trust and freedom to choose and decide on that meaning rather than being a victim of centricity and conformity to go by the majority observation based meaning of the term.

Mental traps prevent the required flow or level of 'eccentricity':
Actually, the original mind and intellect is 'eccentric' or random in their choices and functions. If you are sensitive, you may know that your mind is eccentricity itself. But none of those eccentricities may be expressed or manifested 'outside'. However, creativity, originality, and genius is more or less impossible without eccentricity or 'controlled eccentricity'. If hunger and sexuality can be under controlled expressions, eccentricity too can be controlled. But, the mental traps of conformity, fear of criticism and failure, etc seldom permit the expressions of eccentricity and any inspiration for non-usual behaviour or action, work or dialogues, relationships, etc would be interpreted as eccentricity by one's own mind, and therefore stopped.

Eccentricity does not allow the fear-tension-anxiety about being perceived-labelled-talked about as a 'bad-boy' or 'bad-girl', or do things to ensure entry in the good books of others. Eccentricity does not permit conspicuous consumption, extravagance, and unproductive social-networks. It does not support anxiety-fear of critiques, tension of 'pleasing' others, or worry about low-ness and inferiorities. Of course, children are trained to be good and right by the dialogues of 'What others might think about you?'. Not by explaining the logic of goodness, rightness, and correctness.

Mental traps and 'social perception':
Cognizing, perceiving, and thinking about
the 'others' and their vantage-points

In general, people are okay and moving in life-work-relationships more-or-less smoothly. But if just one variant is toppled, suddenly their balance-of-mind or feelings and emotions are affected.

Somewhat like one wrong word inducing a war between people or nations. Ninety nine good words and deeds are instantly disregarded and sidelined. But of course, the parameters of 'good' are stringent about 'other' persons or people. Just one bad word or deed is not tolerated despite 99 good words and deeds. There could be plenty of violent and bad words and deeds in a trapped mindberg necessitated to manage the fears and tensions of comparison, missing goals and purposes, inferiority feelings, etc. Or when there is a conflict of interests and motives such violent words and deeds come out in the open.

However, good words and appreciation are often restrained even about the most positive experience – the most wonderful ecstatic experience [according to their own claim]. Why? It is again a mental trap. That, one is not supposed to feel good about his self; because, due to training, only deprivation drives survival-sustenance activities. At the same time, the paradox is that, people often disregard the views or vantage-points of the 'others'. For example, the vantage-point used for explaining a certain event or thing, person or phenomenon is enforced on the 'others'.

The same event may be explained in one way by one group or person and some other way by another person or group. One of them may insist on his or view on the other. The universal example is that about the 'God'. There is an assumption that there can be only one God or only one reason or invariant aspect for things. This is supported by the so-called sciences that rigidly insist on one core truth or set of theory that explains everything [of a category or domain of entities, things, and phenomena]. Because of the insistence on the only-one truth, only-one-reason, only-one-fact etc, conflicts occur at all levels of interpersonal relationships. Even in inter-national relations.

As a result of the complex 'fear-tension-anxiety' element of mental traps, everyone is trying to influence the 'other' or 'others'. The all out effort to make the others 'lovable' or 'likeable' or to belong to the same social-network or ideology. So, the mental traps determine the base of social-networks and inter-personal relationships. In other words, 'birds of the same feathers flock together'. [However, high achievers and eccentrics do not flock together - like the mental trapped majority – due to their sense of originality and uniqueness].

Parents, peers, relatives, community, schools, religions, ideologies and so on are all trying to make people ['the others'] 'likeable'. This indirectly proves that the social-networks are based on compatibility of mental traps. The developing child witnesses the significant others interact with 'others' from the vantage-points of:

- social class and economic conditions
- familial and group allegiance
- religious and community membership
- education levels
- role-function or job-work levels
- gender and age classes
- territory-state-location-culture grounds
- political, ideological, normative allegiance

Peace-loving people participate in global peace initiatives by mystics and gurus. The good-correct-right people do not mix with the bad-wrong-incorrect and the vice versa. As a result, the good remains good and the bad, the bad.

Paradoxical effects of 'Medium-High-Severe' mental traps

There is no real communication across people of different levels of mind-sets. For instance, great books and ideas are discussed in networks of individuals of corresponding levels of mind-settings. Please be aware that the 'other side' of mental traps is the 'trap-free process of the mind and intellect'. The mental trapped people cannot tolerate greater levels of ideas.

The complete absence of mental 'blocks', [the absence of 'threshold mental blocks'] is perhaps more negative and dysfunctional than 'severe' mental traps. It is approximately possible that an absolute absence of fears and anxieties of all kinds, absolute eccentricity and non-conformity, absolute flexibility must entail a dangerous antisocial criminal character. Paradoxically, those who are inordinately greedy for power, control, and authority are likely to have 'severe' mental traps.

Mental Traps: Block the 'Happiness Purpose'

The ultimate force of life is towards 'happiness', balance, contentment, fulfilment. But, the mental traps may corrupt relationships, self perception, and activities required for work or economic activities. Out of all, 'relationships' with close linkages, neighbourhood, society, or the others in general are the most decisive factor in sustaining happiness. And precisely that happiness purpose [the evolved state of 'pleasure principle'] get the most affected by mental traps.

Relationships are the most serious foundation mind-set established in the little child. It becomes ever-stronger and supremely reinforced. Perhaps, the entire perspective of 'detachment' is about detaching from relationships. The sound and fury of the tale of life is mostly generated by the pattern of relationships. Why the Rishis and mystics chose to remain relatively aloof from people, especially from marital relationships? Why most of the creative-original and genius individuals remained unmarried or got separated sooner or definitely later?

The increasing rate of divorce is primarily due to the individual difference in centricity-conformity, self-doubt, fear and tension of low-ness, and sensitivity-lag. The core problem with divorce in India is in the way separation is managed. The man or the woman would concoct various stories, false interpretations, and biased explanations and develop a strong thesis of allegations to rationalize the act of separation.

The resource-myopia and self-doubt, anxiety and fear of humiliation [about separation] would drive the person involved in justifying the separation by the power of hatred. Not by the power of clarity of perception about the definitions of difference between them. So, great animosity is sustained, leading to utter conflict in children.

Have a minute of projecting or seeing the facilities available for life, survival-sustenance, etc, mental, intellectual, aesthetic, etc systems available today that are meant for the 'happiness purpose' of life.

Leaders at all levels, rulers, clerics, administrators, etc are equally dissatisfied that their followers or disciples or masses are perpetually unhappy. Employers are unhappy that the employees are unhappy.

The current mass of populations seem to be dissatisfied with life despite amazing facilities created and developed, installed and maintained by the work of dedicated individuals. Water taps inside home, electricity, television, laptop, automobiles, transport, films, dance, music, poetry, fiction, philosophies, and above all the agents and clerics are trying their best to prove the power of gods and so on. Yet the range and degree of dissatisfaction only increases. Really increasing..! More than that of a decade back, much more than that of the rural folks, much more than even the times when none of the so-called scientific-technological wonders existed.

And the ridiculous paradox is that, almost not a single one of those amazing creative people or wonderful geniuses or great mystics and rishis or even glorified deities such as Jesus, Krishna, Buddha, and so on the well-known, was born and brought up in any significantly good or advantageous setting and facilities and comfort zones of life or work or relationships..!

Note:
India ranks 133 in Happiness Index, 2018*
The parameters included: inequality, life expectancy, GDP per capita, social freedom, generosity, public trust [lack of corruption in government and business], and social support. Pakistan is ranked 75 and China 86; Bhutan 97, Bangladesh 115, and Sri Lanka 116 - the neighbours. Quite probable that India ranks number one in the incidence of mental traps..!

*World Happiness Report is an annual report published
  by the UN Sustainable Development Solutions Network

Mental Traps and the basic triad of Choice-Decision-Action in life, work, relationships.

One crucial aspect of mental traps is that, they interfere with the choices one makes in life, work, relationships; decisions, and actions. More traps at the decision-points and much more traps around the corner of actions or 'doings'. Mental traps block decisions of the 'doings' essential for the development of the 'being'. For instance, an idea may be chosen out of several ones and even genuinely believed: 'Love your neighbour', or 'Satyam Eva Jayate', or 'stealing and bribery is unethical': no mental traps. But to actually do it, plenty of mental traps. Entire populations accept the ethical norms and values of their environment, religion, culture, tradition, etc. Publicly espouse them. But their mental traps do not permit them to live in accordance with them..! Because of mental traps, self-analysis is seldom done. **There is the fear and tension to analyze oneself.**

Reflect and observe one's own expressions, responses, actions, behaviours, dialogues, work, and relationships. Be dangerously truthful to oneself. If impossible to introspect and reflect upon and analyse oneself, then don't just observe but reflect and creatively think about life around. Examples everywhere.

Mental traps make you a mere 'statistical person'
Not an 'indivisible individual'
[The term individual refers to 'a distinctive or original person'..!]

Due to the mental trap of fear-tension-anxiety of humiliation, alienation, low-ness, etc in general, the Statistical-Indian cannot tolerate just another person coming up in wealth, fame, acceptance, competence, better role position, etc. Because, it induces a subtle sense of humiliation by the 'comparison-analysis' process.

The increasing competency of the other person [especially of a known or familiar person], is perceived as a 'threat' to the self image [duplicated one]. The artificial uniqueness is affected. Above all, the mental trap of fear of low-ness is triggered.

The 'affected' individual or individuals would form network to defeat or put down the newly emerging success stories. There are plenty in the myths and folklores. Across traditions and places in India. Buddha chased out of India. The Indian Gurukula system is rendered obsolete. The great Rishis and Mystics of India are not listened to and genuinely accepted as models of life and self and relationships. Indian history is filled with examples of the manifestations of the mental traps.

By the mental trap of 'low-ness' and 'inferiority-complex', the 'identity' becomes vague and sporadic. Social, religious, economic, political affiliations and allegiance too are sometimes used to define the identity. The very meaning of the term 'individual' is not investigated vis-a-vis oneself. By the mental trap of 'low-ness' or inferiority feeling, the comparison-analysis process works in a dysfunctional way for the already trapped condition.

Every time you take a 'prasadam', see yourself as a different entity eating it. You become the guest of honor of the deity. The 'pujari' had converted your offering, 'cooking' it in the energy field of mantras and 'homams' created inside the sanctum sanctorum. The principle behind that practice is to be 'grasped'. Not a mere act of centricity and conformity. In other words, the human being that eats the 'prasadam' must be a shifted entity – to become eligible to take it. Or during taking it. So too smearing of sandal paste or 'bhasma', etc. So 'doing' it about ninety times a standard human being should be reaching complete tuning. If not, there must be some eugenics trap.

By centricity-conformity at the non-conscious of the mindberg human beings become 'old aged' - of course, in their mind-setting, in their self-image, self-description. The physical senses have to conform to the obvious evidences of the physical body withering away gradually. It is a core nature reality. Plants, birds, and lions become old aged. Of course, in their 'body'. Physical matter is very vulnerable to variations and atrophy. The energies of the mind, intellect, and spirit just cannot get 'old'.
Of course, if there is freedom from the mental traps.
Undoubted freedom from the fear, panic, tension, anxiety.

A rose is a rose is a rose and a cat is a cat is a cat.

Human beings often despise animals, use 'animal' as a derogatory term. Compare evil, bad, criminal, naming unethical deeds as animalistic behavior, lower-than-animals, etc. Is that correct?

It implies that animals are ignorant about the norms, values, principles, etc. Certainly, animals, every one of the varied species, are firm-correct-elegant-taoic and complete in whatever their 'knowings' and 'doings' and 'states-of-being' whether they have norms and rules or not.

Every cat is a cat is a cat. There are no ignorant cats. Fully and completely and correctly they do their 'doings' by their 'knowing' – whatsoever. And, that's their quality of firm, correct, elegant, taoic, completeness. Genius or 'attendant spirit' or 'swa' is firm, correct, elegant, complete, taoic, and complete.

So, human beings of injurious character are simply ignorant. But is it so? In fact, the one who violate principles only know the principles more clearly so that they can plan their violations. Actually, they do it only because of the mental traps of a complex pattern.

The '**pattern**' of mental traps is more critical. For instance, great and unmanageable fear-tension-anxiety about life as a high mental trap on one side and close to threshold self-doubt and resource-myopia on the other side. Out of their desperation of suffering from fear, tension, and anxiety they venture into the intimidating behaviors and actions empowered by their self-confidence and power of resources.

Cats have gods? Birds and plants have gods? As everything about cats and birds is programmed then their perception of god also must be elegant-complete-correct-taoic-firm. In tune with the spirit or genius. They are just there: eating when hungry, sleeping when the feel so. The way the supreme Zen Master defined Zen: 'I eat when I am hungry'. The way the supreme Zen Master defined Zen: 'I eat when I am hungry'. No familiarity traps. Because, no self-importance trap. No speed-traps: complete calmness, no internal turbulence.

Mental Traps and Self-Discovery

Those who have really attempted discovering their 'self' as the core driver of the entity; they might understand the concept and reality of mental traps because of their own experiences [working as 'evidences'].

Your enlightenment or Satori, of course, you may try. But it has to occur by its own sweet uncertain point of time completely in line with the design-setting of your mind, intellect, and attendant spirit.
That cannot be consciously invoked.

The 'gate-less gate' cannot be opened by any planned set of movements. That too movements in the subtle realms. No great poet can decide to write a poem just by conscious decision or by the invitation by someone. Like balance on the cycle cannot be consciously managed to access. It may occur as you continue to behave with the bicycle. But the attendant-spirit or the Double is not a material design like the bicycle. The phi-phenomenon is absolutely subtle and your actions to get at it too must be equally subtle. A sort of action-less action. The gate-less gate is to be trespassed.

The very desire for Satori itself may carry linkages with certain mental traps: rigidity or self-doubt or centricity and fear or tension of failure in life or 'actual' failure and defeat in life or work or relationships [by sort of 'evidences']. That is, you are directing your attention to something called Satori about which you have no idea or clarity of intent.

Fear of ambiguity may work in the non-conscious. The end may not justify the means. How can one search consciously for something that is absolutely unknown and untested before?

The acts of 'searching the fugitive by beating the drums' cannot work. The great Krishna had to talk for days to Arjuna to convince him to taking arms against the blood relations. Finally Krishna even had to sort of threaten Arjuna by revealing his universe-level format.

Mental traps and families, institutions, governments, organizations

The mental traps manifested in individuals get automatically reflected and represented in the responses, actions, relationships, languages, etc of families, groups, institutions, organizations, nations, and governments. Mental traps define the relations between nations or the attitudes and positions taken by the leaders of the nations.

As the parents and others carry mental traps, children are trained or forced and guided to imitate, duplicate, and adopt responses, behaviours, and actions that are comfortable and convenient for them. Teachers induce traps to students, and so on. It seems that, the majority of Indian institutions, organizations, and governance centres would prefer to have people with a lot of mental traps - unconsciously. By the ways of reports about Indian organizations, and research experience with some of them, mostly private sector organizations with a global outlook, especially globally competitive institutions and governments might expect a critical mass of people with low mental traps.

The consequences of mental traps for India: Tremendous. Vicious spiral.

If the nature of mental traps is understood from this book, drive your engines of analytic reflection for an hour and find out how the mental traps are linkaged with the events, people, and related familial, social, religious, economic, cultural, political phenomena in India. Perhaps, anyone connected with Corporate India must differentiate the subtle ways in which the mental traps retard the possible-probable shift from the usual -to- good and 'good -to- great'.

- The terrible lapses in the bureaucratic functions of the governance and other core systems. Bribery and corruption. Perpetual 'red-tape' phenomena.
- Lower than the possible level of outputs and outcomes. Inconsistent quality of Indian products and services.
- Adulterated food items, vegetables.
- Poor quality work climate and interpersonal relationship culture.

134

- Absolute lack of innovation or creativity. People work by their 'appointment orders' - not by inspiration, dedication, commitment, and sense of ownership. In general, almost all anomalies of institutions and organizations must be due to the salience of mental traps of the participating members. Students learn by sheer necessity alone - not by inspiration and will.

Mental Traps of the leaders-managers of education system: Disregard for the core purpose of education

India is a signatory in the UN Convention* on the Rights of Child. [*2nd September 1990]. In the charter on the 'Aim of Education', Article 29 states thus:
"Education shall aim at developing the child's personality, talents, and mental and physical abilities to the fullest extent."

India is a land of supreme perspectives about education.
For instance, Swami Vivekananda said:
"If I had to do my education once again, I would not study facts at all. I would develop the **power of concentration** and **detachment**, and then with a perfect instrument collect facts at will." [**bold added**]
[The complete works of Swami Vivekananda,
Mayavati Memorial Edition, Advaitashram, 1952, pages. 28, 366]

SEE, Table 11 below Showing the average percentage of mental traps of three critical orbits of teachers

	MS1	MS2	MS3	MS4	MS5	MS6	MS7
College Teachers							
[N:124]	38.2	30.6	32.5	26.0	24.0	33.4	32.7
B-School Teachers							
[N: 26]	51.0	43.6	49.2	35.3	36.7	42.6	47.0
School Teachers							
[N: 456]	52.5	41.6	41.3	30.1	27.6	40.5	42.0

Special Note on the Linkages of Creativity, Originality, Genius with the Mental traps

In fact, the concept of Mental Block is most commonly used by researchers in creativity, originality, and genius. [This book itself is based on the mental blocks differentiated by Pradip N Khandwalla in his book, 'The Fourth Eye']. The presence of mental blocks-traps in anyone can be differentiated by any experienced researcher in mind-sets. Of course, a statistical percentage cannot be attributed to such observations. The PNK-Questionnaire is a tool to get a statistically ascertained extent and pattern of mental blocks-traps.

The researchers in creativity unanimously agree that mental traps prevent the possible-probable creativity and genius of human beings. And at the same time, researchers agree that there is creativity in every human being.

Yes, one of the clearest evidences of the creativity of human beings is in the way the mental blocks-traps restrict that very creativity..! The ingenious ways in which ambiguous, unclear, uncertain, strange, and new things and ideas are averted or escaped from. How the 'others' are humiliated without any evidences, how actions are sustained in their functional fixedness, how one's own inspirations are repressed, in managing insensitivities; in using language to make others low or glorify and deify the geniuses so that the Freudian defenses are beautifully practised, and so on.

The way the mental traps operate in restricting or governing the responses, behaviors, actions, and dialogues of people is actually an expression of high creativity or originality. For instance, the maid instantly stops all her drama and expressions with her friend as soon as the master of the house appears in the distant corner.
As he approaches, her entire body shrugs into an obvious appearance of 'low-ness' - especially if she belongs to a low community. Even the expressive movements of the body, or posture, or facial expressions etc are vulnerable to the intervention of mental blocks-traps.
Such manifestations are driven by the mental blocks-traps.

136

Much before entering the space of uncertainty, or failure, or humiliation, the individual would have already turned away from them. Even before the turning point comes, the vehicle would be steered far away - mostly non-consciously. That too is creativity. Creativity is 'domain specific'. The nature of creativity required for dance is different from that of music and drama or film making. Creativity in poetry and in fiction are different. And so on. So, creativity is in management and genius in leadership are to be in tune with requirements of organizations and institutions, ideologies and governments, and so on.

Every child is 'creative'..?

No child is creative at birth. Mind is empty. Intellect engines are just waiting in 'idling' conditions. Yet, every child carries the potentialities or the entelechy to be creative. A child can talk a language – by eliciting, refining, and shaping its sounding potential. Not spontaneously. It is the case with creativity. At the core of all creative process there are the engines the mind, intellect, and spirit working. What else?

If the so-called 'every child' is creative, then what is the block? Where the 'every child' disappeared in the 'adult world' of India?

- How the 'every child' ends up in the crowd of societies?
- Where is the creativity, originality, and genius of India?
- Why India is not able to differentiate talents and still trapped by narrow fears-tensions-anxieties of inferiorities and go by the sensitivity-lag about evidences?

As of now, almost every modern educated-intelligent parent declares this 'duplicated knowing' that 'every child is creative'. But the parent seldom tries to verify the so-called creative-ness of their child. The don't try to know at least the nature of creativity in its rudimentary projections possible in a child. It is duplication because, they never examined the nature of creativity or the way creativity is expressed in its beginning stages in their child, the mind-sets or attributes of creativity, the requirements for developing it, the way feedback to be given, and so on.

See, the population of mental trapped people are parents too..!
Their mental traps induce and nurture mental traps in children.

The mental traps of parents invariably reflect in their intimate interfaces
with the child. The teachers sow new seeds of linkages that expand the
mental traps in children during about 2,000+ class-room days.
The media, films, myths, traditions all together do a real creative
campaign that reinforce the basic emotions of fear-tension-anxiety in
children. Especially through using ideas and imageries about so-called
'death'. The 'fear of death': the core of all fears.

Population of students and learners are not aware of the details
of the way creativity and genius actually work or exist in their entities.
The text books are all about the output-outcomes of creativity and
originality. But not about how to develop it. There are about 35+
techniques on triggering creativity or for problem-solving. None of
them is a topic in schools or even in higher university courses or in
the B-Schools, nor a topic of training programs in corporations and
governments. The creativity of mental traps is such that it is creative in
stopping even the genius of the attendant spirit. They have the power to
kill and destroy those linkages that threaten their states and statements.

Everybody is 'creative'..?

Of course, the entire community of researchers in creativity declared that
'everybody is creative'. It is a truth. But it is like saying that every hand has
all its possible-probable movements. That does not mean that it will play
on the tabla or violin without the creative inspiration to differentiate that
unique set of movements from out of the random potential movements
required for playing Tabla or Piano, Calligraphy or Piano, Veena or
Guitar, etc. Everyone enjoys music or film songs. NO training is essential.
It denotes the presence of music in everyone. But the unconscious mental
traps would not allow them to try it out. It requires the movement of
musical sensitivity, sense for rhythm, speed, and tune. It requires the
spirit or will to practice so that the relevant movements
are reinforced and stabilized.

Sadly, the mind-sets that drive creativity and originality and genius are never trained or induced by the environment – especially of India. In rare situations a child may coincidently undergo experiences that invoked certain creative motivation and related mind-sets. If everybody is creative, that creativity is for discovering the originality of the entity, genius; getting enlightened. Satori. Not to do music or dance, not for innovation in work, or painting, etc.

The movement of the engines-of-intellect are capable of grasping any reality and its core principles. The spirit, the Double of the entity can be tuned into the consciousness. In reality, every human entity must carry the engine speeds to function at the so-called levels of creativity and originality and genius. But seldom the mind is 'free-wheeling' or the intellect is 'free-floating' to be sensitive to those extra movements and carry the power of spirit to enter into those 'mental trap' prevented domains of entelechies. The mental traps block entelechy [identifying and developing the potentialities of the human 'cat'].

The so-called creativity and originality and genius of the so-called 'everybody' can be in the very expressions, responses, behaviours, actions, and dialogues. In self, life, work, and relationships of usual survival-sustenance environments. In fact, the ultimate of creativity is in discovering the originality of one's 'being'. For achieving self-realization, for enlightenment, for Satori.

The choice to do something and the decision to actually act or try doing it is blocked in between by the deep mental traps. Not realising that truth, individuals engage in various ego-defense mechanisms and feel justified about their incompleteness. There is great desire or claim of uniqueness - not one of the crowd. But most decisions and actions are of the crowd mind-set, by the crowd mind-set, and for the crowd ['centricity-conformity'].

The 'Make in India' Campaign and the Mental Traps

The government has been campaigning the need for creativity in the guise of 'Make in India'. But it just cannot work. This campaign with all its great intent is near impossible to get translated into reality. Because, the great majority of educated populations are far remote in the mind-setting, intellect, and spirit required to do the 'doing' of Make in India.

In other words, populations were not waiting for any campaign to become creative...! They are incapable of being creative and original despite their desire for it. The so-called 'National Innovation Council' [NIC] could not do anything significant. There were declarations and seminars and conferences on behalf of 'Innovation Decade' 2011-2020. There is no short cuts and gimmicks and rote methods about creativity and genius.

The Females and Mental Traps

As mentioned before, the mental traps and linkaged mind-sets are formed from the environment. The typical Indian environment is very conducive to training, teaching, and guidance in forming the mental traps to females also. Quite probable in slightly more doses than to males. Therefore, this section.

According to the data of B-School students, the mental traps of females are relatively higher than those of the males. See Table 12 below:

	MS1	MS2	MS3	MS4	MS5	MS6	MS7
FEMALES MBA							
[N: 781]	**48.1**	**41.3**	**42.5**	**34.9**	**30.6**	**42.4**	**42.5**
MALES MBA							
[N: 773]	44.7	38.7	35.8	31.0	26.0	41.0	38.8
FEMALES University Students							
[N: 2,699]	51.3	30.2	46.7	35.7	32.1	40.6	46.7
MOTHERS							
[N: 129]	**58.8**	**50.2**	**55.1**	**41.1.**	**35.2**	**48.7**	**41.6**

The very definition of the female is based on the mental trap of centricity and conformity of the male world-view and perspectives about human beings and their attributed characteristics. Of course, the males too are trapped in the centricity-conformity definitions about the male-ness or masculinity. This in turn, induce mental traps about males in the mindbergs of the females.

The God is referred-to as a male. Evidence: the use of 'He'. Religions and social, familial, political, economic, developmental, administrative perspectives are all defined by men. Women are trained to be in centricity-conformity with those perspectives. Trained at home, by peers, media, school, workplace and traditions - all defined by men.

The females have achieved freedom and economic liberation. But not existential freedom. They are terribly trapped in the male centricity-conformity driven world view and female-view. Most of the work settings, including the very democratically elected governments are of the typically masculine mind-sets. However, being trained in the male world view, the attitudes of the females could be the duplication and imitation of men's ways of responses, behaviours, actions, dialogues, and work. Despite possible-probable internal disagreement with the masculine mechanical world-view and female-view which is unlikely to be talked outside due to, again, the very mental traps.

The females do not tend to unite with firm completeness especially because of their menta-traps of fear-tension-anxiety of low-ness that is derived from the non-conscious comparison with other females. There is a non-conscious deep attachment with the body and its youthful elegance provided by the design-setting and process of the nature, though.

Reportedly, significant percent of males take bribes because of the mental traps of their wives. Their mental traps about tension-anxiety of future, of lowness, uncertainty, self doubt, etc compensated by possessing gold, savings, wealth generation, etc. To manage 'low-ness' they enter into severe load of gossiping, campaigns of jealousy and envy, and disregard for their own community. Their perceived low-ness is compensated by demand for equality with men: to adopt the expressions, responses, actions, behaviours, dialogues, work, etc like that of men. Instead of demanding 'equalization of their difference' from men. Instead of establishing their philosophies and perspectives, world-views and self-views as of equal value and completeness, firmness and correctness as that of men.

Therefore, man created a lot of familial, social, economic conflicts and wars, aggressive encroaches and subjugations, conquered helpless populations and enslaved them in order to protect the females. Similarly, quite possible-probable that the acts and works and relationships of corruption, bribery, food adulteration, crimes, loot, murder, and such kind of male atrocities are conceived mainly for the sake of the female.

A local proverb says that the majority of 'problems and conflicts in life are due to women and gold'. So, the females seem to enjoy the situation that they remain as a top mental trap for the male. And that mental trap sustains the continuity of the species, though.

The females induce and enforce mental-blocks-traps in children. First, in the form of the mother, then lady teachers*** in schools. The mothers use the logic of making a 'wonderful child' and teachers a 'brilliant student' - using strategies of mental trap induction by threats, warnings, punishments, etc.

> ***Teachers: As of now, at least 90 percent of teachers in the KG, primary, and high school levels must be females. Their mental traps are very likely to manifest in their language, in their treatment of students, ways on expressions, responses, behaviours, actions, use of language, and relationships to students. Schools by very design-setting are meant for implementing mental traps in children. And that work seems to be effectively performed by the lady teachers.

Discipline problems are increasing directly contradicting increasing regulations and conditions enforced in schools and at home. Children are resorting to alcohol, drugs, and deviant behaviours because of the expanded anxiety about future and life in the future in general.

Several of the 'socialized' acts [for recognition and appreciation', possessions of richness and wealth, power and control etc] of men might carry linkages with mental traps having orbits of reference groups comprising the females than the male counterparts. Of course, by frequency and nature of incidence of events, it seems that the males carry an extra mental trap having linkages with females – directly or indirectly [for example, of anxiety of losing the love, affection, assistance, support etc of the woman].

+++
The mental traps of the 'Mothers' and 'Lady Teachers', the most critical to be resolved. The logic is clear.

Females: Yet, a Paradox of Mental Traps

However, a paradox: the females have greater control over their mental traps. If they decide, they can switch off the functions of almost every mental trap of fear-tension-anxiety, assume immense flexibility and functional variation, and develop great sensitivity in a short time. IN training programs and short workshops, consistently, the female respondents revealed greater shifts in perspective and quicker resolution or transcendence of mental traps than the males. Perhaps, because, their mental traps are peripheral duplications and imitations whereas the mental traps of males are induced and enforced more strongly and reinforced more frequently as they get involved in the activities of social, religious, economic, political, familial, group, social-network domains.

The females are ready to change their stance in life, work, relationships, and responses-behaviors-actions. In radical ways. The female just decides to live with a man - mostly, the man chooses-decides the female, though. Theoretically a perfect state of freedom from the mental-block of fear-tension-anxiety of the unknown and ambiguous. No fear-tension-anxiety of failure or of humiliation or of low-ness. But, such jumps are also because, of the power of centricity-conformity [as well as insistence by powerful others and requirements of survival-sustenance]. All their mind-sets of mental-blocks-traps remain intact and become more active. Therefore, they insist and drive their men to undertake anything to salvage them from the centricity-conformity driven fears, tensions, and anxieties. [Centricity-conformity driven fear-and-anxiety, generated by stories of penury and tribulation if weak in money, savings, wealth, etc].

Evidence:
Conventionally, a girl living under the safety and security of her family is one day ready to leave her safety zone to go to her husband's place and adjust. For a man it would trigger mental traps 1, 3, and 4. That is a nature-process driven speciality of the female of the species because they are the ones to adapt with the males – by default. That is why the demand for 'equality with men' [rather than demanding identical status for their difference].

However, the future trends indicate a shift in paradigm. In the conventional times, even, they were just ready to accept a new man into their life and leave all close loving relationships and be a part of the husband's time-space-location and people relationships settings.

With all kinds of centricity-conformity they are ready to shift to sometimes a totally different set of values, attitudes, perspectives, ways of responses-behaviors-actions; dialogues, work, and ways of relationships. Just by one day. Whereas a man would find it complex to adjust and adapt with the settings of the space, relationships, etc of the wife's location. Studies reveal that wives outlive the husbands, in general. But, certainly, females in the domain of creative expressions: arts, crafts, poetry, fiction, dance, theatre, film, painting, music, etc were found to retain their eccentricity or trap-free mind. In fact, much more firmly and clearly than men of similar fields.

All the mental traps may exist in a female. But at any point of time she is just ready to jump into the uncertain, ambiguous, strange, unknown, and new – of existence process. She can see without looking. They are capable of great humility and commitment. They are not trapped in religions and rituals as the men seem to be. They have the power to look at reality from different vantage-points. Every time a female goes out to public time-space-locations she is managing her mental traps. In her workplaces also. Therefore, though their mental traps are little higher than those of the males, they are far better managers of their minds despite traps.
So, females are historically the great spies.

With all the mental traps, females have the power to shift their perspective of life, work, and relationships. If the man becomes defeated and disillusioned, the woman provides sense of direction and limitless support and encouragement - as if they are beyond all mental traps. She is capable of climbing the Everest of existence despite shivering heart. In many villages and remote areas of India, they manage the survival and sustenance of their husbands and children. If they resolve their mental traps, then, even the sky may not delimit them.

So, the adage: 'Behind every successful man, there is a woman'. Perhaps, now it is time that whatever they did to ensure the success of their men, they may do so to themselves too. Of course, with greater purposes and goals than mere duplication of the mind-setting of the Newtonian* mechanical world-view.

[* the term duplicated from the books, 'The Tao of Physics' and 'The Turning Point' by Particle Physicist-Mystic Fritjof Capra]

Females and the Vision-of-the-Future

There is a great wonder in the vision-of-future defined by Sidney J Parnes, Past Chairman of the Board, Creative Education Foundation, USA:

> "I look to future centuries of self-actualizing individuals, whose main purpose in life is self-actualizing themselves and helping others do the same (children, families, students, employees, friends, colleagues) to ever higher levels of an infinite continuum of human potential development ... blended with self-healing programs carrying thousands toward levels attained in the past by only a handful of saints or gurus... People will move toward self-help from institutional help as Naisbitt predicted as one of the ten "Megatrends". They will be empowered by their own abilities."*
> [* Journal of Creative Behaviour, Vol. 21, No. 4, Fourth Quarter, 1987, pp 297-298, bold added]

Females and Attention-to-details: By default, the female of the species is capable of greater sharpness of attention. Perhaps, the females can take up the lead; they can decide to define a new 'genius-loci' for India by focusing attention to their domain of people and life-work-activities.

The genius-loci of India can be changed only by the genius of the females. They have the power to make quick shifts much more than the men. They shall not stop a the boundaries of their mental traps. They may create even new social, religious, political, educational, and governance ideologies instead of rigidly following and working for the philosophies and perspectives of the masculine world-view. Why not?

Mental Traps and
the Genius-Loci of India
Genius Loci: The prevailing character of a place

So, the genius-loci of India is nothing but manifestations of the fears, tensions, and anxieties of uncertainty and failure, future and complexities; anxiety of lowness; self-doubt and resource myopia; rigidities and functional fixities; and severe lag in creative sensitivities - despite being a great country of art, craft, music, dance, theatre, literature, etc.

Now that you've got a grasp of the nature of mental traps, develop your clarity about the pervasive presence of them in the Indian social processes, Indian education, Indian governance offices, Indian business organizations, and Indian families.

The political leaders are likely to carry their pattern of mental traps, clerics carry theirs, and traders carry theirs. Not much of 'Satyameva Jayate'. No genuine dedicated commitment to the people and a sense for their unspoken troubles.

Power and control oriented leaders would tend to perpetuate the mental traps of populations under their influence. They may try to induce anxiety of uncertainty and future, self-doubt and resource myopia in the voting populations. The campaigns are singularly focussed on the deep non-conscious mind-set of centricity
and conformity.

India apparently retains its originality to an extent. Sustains its genius-loci suggested by the great mystics and Rishis or the myths and legends of history. So, a critical mass of so-called Hindus almost follow the 'aham brahmasmi' or 'god is everywhere', or feel confident about their trust in a deity such as Shiva or Durga or Kali or Saraswati or Rama or Krishna, Hanuman or Tripurasundari, and so on. They consider the very body as a temple [yet taken-for-granted, though].

As a result, they are very tolerant to any questions raised against such beliefs [as superstition or personal god, etc]. Seldom would a Hindu be bothered about whether other Hindus followed the same religion or rituals. And so on. Anyone can analytically see that. Luckily this immensity of flexibility and variations of sensitivities was facilitated:

- by the absence of a singular only-one god or deity as the supreme Head,
- no central 'book' [such as Bible or Koran etc] to establish the logic and interpretations of the linkages that define the one-ness of that central god,
- no leaders-managers to coordinate or organize the population transcending the historical division-separation and differentiation of 'Áham Brahmasmi' + 'Vasudhiva Kudumbakam'; the related several stories and myths and evidences entailing mostly an escapist's openness to other ideologies.

The well-organized religions define even the identity of nations based on their ideologies and world-views. Driven by such intents, they started propagating their gods and relevant perspectives at other space-locations too. Ample evidences by the number of wars and genocides. By the lack of integration of the varied populations of the so-called Hindus, and the resultant mental traps of self doubt and centricity-conformity, such powerful religions could get entry and conversion.

In India, the normal population imitate or duplicate the expressions, responses, behaviors, dialogues, and actions and ways of relationships of the 'upper' classes because of the fear, or tension, or anxiety of 'low-ness' and inferiority feelings.

It is nothing but the high levels of fears-and-anxieties of the divided-separated-subdued communities that rendered the task of the invaders easy. That differentiation-division-separation is the tragedy of India. Generating and sustaining the vicious spiral of mental traps in such a grand majority.

In India centricity-conformity carries heavy lot of critical linkages of social consequences. In fact, the entire design and setting and process of caste system in India is around the mental trap of centricity-conformity. Great majority of people strongly follow the centricity-conformity suggested by the CEOs and HR managers and Marketing-Managers of religions and communities. More or less the same way political ideologies are managed for selecting rulers.

Leaders and managers give discourses about the freedom to make opinions, to provide suggestions, reviews and comments etc. But if the comment is against the vested interests, then they are unwelcome, and attacked, or defended. Knowing this 'culture', nobody makes any 'negative comment' even when things are really going worse. Everyone pretends that everything is fine. Mental traps force the tendency to maintain insensitivity and comfort zones. Nobody does manipulation and embezzlement food adulteration, etc for basic survival-sustenance. Corruption and manipulation is done not by the BPL populations.

What you see most salient in the Indian environment is the 'taken-for-granted' attitude and 'self-importance'. People, especially the poor population; environment [of course, the 'Swacha Bharat Mission' is a great initiative], administration [requires a lot of 'cleansing'], public service, production and distribution of things for the poor population; schooling and education, children, women, etc are all victims of the taken-for-granted attitude. Equally held by the rich and the poor, powerful and the powerless, men and women and children.
The 'familiarity-trap': it is an old country. The jasmines have been in the centuries old courtyards. 'Foreign' anything is more appetising and alluring. Of course, the foreign anythings are good quality as they are not produced by people and governments with the 'taken-for-granted' attitude.

Quite fitting to self-doubt and resource myopia, there is the perpetual expression of 'self-importance'. Perhaps, 'aham brahmasmi' and 'ayam atma brahma' and personalised deities must have contributed to that supreme sense of self-importance. Instead of genuine 'self-respect'.

Self-importance is manifested mostly, subtly, some times expressed vigorously if triggered in close interactions of any conflicting context. No sense of gratitude.

Self-importance, defined by:
- one's field of 'knowing', general-knowledge,
- norms of responses, behaviours, actions, and dialogues
- ways of life-work-relationships
- ideologies, beliefs, attitudes, notions about people, events, signals, things, events, entities, and phenomena.

In fact, the debates, arguments, quarrels and conflicts or even aggressive behaviours and acts are primarily due to self-importance.

In India, most people choose subjects, institutions, study well, improve things and details of settings, and develop social-network mainly for creating-maintaining that self-importance. Not basically due to inspiration and love for a subject matter or career. And 'identity' is based on the jobs, designations, possessions - just a parallel orbit of linkages of the caste division-separation based treatment.

Parents and peers pester students to try professional courses for raising self-importance – not by their liking and competency. Good learners try for certain jobs based on the possible-probable scope of self-importance that can be achieved with therefore, given mind-sets abilities and education. Having only the learning certificates they get into jobs and role functions and they fumble. Okay, after joining the job of high consequences for the institution and people, again the sense of self-importance [on one side and the mental traps on the other], induce that detachment from the realities of the dependent populations. The extent of that 'detachment' depend upon the disparity between competency and role requirements.

When the mental trap of self-importance becomes high and extreme; coupled with rigidity, sensitivity-lag, fear-tension-anxiety of failure and loss; and fear and anxiety of low-ness; then the evils, or traitors and such scale of criminals are formed in a country with majority comprising the poor, poorest of poor, and marginalised population. The super 'scams' of various types are an evidence. Of course, all kinds of unethical activities are driven by medium-high-severe mental traps only.

Individuals with high-mental traps tend to develop linkages of unethical antisocial, cunning schemes and strategies to influence political, religious, social, economic, institutional leaders. But the positive elements or the counter fields somehow sustain the tilting balance from collapse. The opposition in democracy, the law and order or justice system. But if nation leaders go high in such mental trap setting, depending upon the design of other mind-sets [of cunningness and centricity-conformity with the reference group etc] then such nation leaders can vitiate the life and survival-sustenance of people locally and globally in small or large scale.

To make the genius loci of India a great one:
Be a Creative Manager or Genius Leader

The first and the only critical step to become a creative manager or genius leader: Differentiation and resolution of mental traps - if any.

Be a magical in your time-space-location. Wherever it is.
By being elegant, firm, taoic [in good tune with the realities of existence of oneself and the other entities], and complete the brilliant balance on the internal bicycle of genius [attendant spirit, 'swa' - that 'other self' which is firmly resting on the good, right, and correct in life, work, and relationships] is certainly possible. And it is possible, of course, only by transcending the mental traps as the first requirement. Almost anyone can escape from mental traps. After all, the mental traps are not **metal**-straps.

It is extremely required: the political, social, and religion leaders; administrators, managers-leaders-employees of all corporate entities, B-Schools, etc need to self analyse their mental traps.

151

What is the logic that corporate India needs to be liberated
from mental traps?

The logic:
The entire range of survival-sustenance and life of contemporary and
future world depend upon the expressions, responses, behaviours,
actions, and ideas of the few human beings that comprise corporate
India. The 'doing' and 'state-of-being' of India is so poor and under-
performing only because of the mental traps of the people in corporate
India. What else?

In India, by tradition and culture of deities and worships, and rituals
[though mostly, seemingly, driven by the engines of the mental traps of
centricity-conformity], the population stops at searching for blessings and
blessings and blessings. There does not seem to be a correlated level of
'doings'. Equally, the blessings of gurus and sages etc too are sought
after in complete earnestness and sincerity - especially during the
event of seeking blessing.

A great and supreme act of accepting a guru or an ideology, yet there is
no living by that. The details of this paradox are the work of art of the
mental traps only. The leaders of religions, the mystics and gurus of
spiritual ranges, trainers and teachers, are in love with the continuity
of their sermons and guidance, teachings and blessings... Absolutely
unaware of the hidden mental traps of populations.
Or taking them for granted.

The implications of mental traps are incredibly vast and complex.

+++
The tabla or sitar or guitar must be in elegant-complete-correct-taoic-
firm 'state-of-being' when the Master relates with it. Not subservient and
scared and stupefied by the wonder of the master. Indian mind-sets are
like that. The tabla must be in full completeness in tuning and engines.
Otherwise the master will not – rather cannot touch it. IN other words,
when the tabla is ready the master will start playing it.

The Trap-Free Mind and Intellect

The sentence given in quotes below is from the <u>concluding paragraph of a brilliant creative review of the history</u> of research on 'creativity and genius' by Robert W Weisberg [2006, page 598].

"Perhaps the difference between the greats, the near-greats, and the unknowns is that the greats more than other people, <u>want</u> to be great." [underline added]

Therefore, those who want to be great must first of all examine their mental traps and resolve them. This is our addition to the declaration of Weisberg.

The 'trapped-mind' versus the 'free mind'

Great lot of literature, discourses, and conversations on enlightenment. But what is the rate of success or effectiveness? The Rishis, Mystics, and Gurus have clearly defined, explained, interpreted with parables, metaphor, and hundreds of examples about the nature of reality, the core of human beings, ways of enlightenment and the n-number of possibilities hiding everywhere for Satori. The audience likes to hear the familiar and known concepts and ideas about the gods, pleasing ideas about enlightenment, etc. A good orchestra on film songs is enjoyed. But seldom a song is practised by the majority of the audience.

New sermons about ethics and integrity in work, life, relationships etc are incessantly repeated with virtually no consequences. The media business is thriving on sensational stories of violations of the fundamentals of coexistence. Ethics has become the campaign of life – that much of corruption at several levels of life, work, and relationships. The ardent followers and disciples are not able to do the doing of their great knowings from the religion books and leaders – because of the mental traps. They have faithfully and confidently chosen their gods and deities. They have even taken decisions [to act] according to the sermons and commandments.

But unfortunately it requires free-wheeling engines of the mind and empowered engines-of-intellect to do the decided act.

It is somewhat like the boy who has chosen a girl out of the several, decided to abide by his feeling of love. Decided to marry her. But to do the act of marrying her may require a lot of planning and support or a different level of confidence and capabilities – especially if the affair involves social, economic, religious, etc kind of complexities. Choices are easy. Decisions are tough, because decisions inevitably involve the need for actions, which inevitably requires a trap-free mind-setting and powerful intellect engines of analysis, discussion, conclusions, and recommendations. Decisive actions upon one's own most familiar taken-for-granted self.

How to develop the trap-free mind and intellect?

First of all, develop the inspiration to be a cat of human entity:
        to be creative, original, or genius in responses,
        behaviours, actions, work, relationships and dialogues.
Second of all, identify the trapping mind-sets.
Third of all, resolve or transcend them fully knowing the 'why'
        or the purpose and philosophy of why doing it..

Implications of the key-word: Free
- not under the control or in the power of another;
- able to act or be done as one wishes
- not or no longer confined or imprisoned; not a slave
- able or permitted to take a specified action
- not physically restrained, obstructed, or fixed; unimpeded
- able to occur in or to be isolation
- not subject to or constrained by engagements or obligations
- not subject to or affected by (a specified thing, typically an undesirable one)
- frank or unrestrained in speech, expression, or action
- the concept and idea of 'free-mind'

A 'trap-free mind' is perhaps the most essential requirement for individuals who want to become great, who want to became great managers and genius leaders. Even for enlightenment and Satori. The 'free mind' tends to float naturally closer to the original-mind. Because a 'free mind' is not restricted by the mental traps of fear of the unknown and new nor depressed by challenges and failures.

The 'free mind' is not trapped inside rigidities of thought and analysis. Then, the resultant cognition and perception are original. If there can be the actions of homicide and fratricide and war, various unethical acts and violences on behalf strong decisions, why not the other way round? Is it not blocked only by the pervasive mental traps and mental traps only? What else?

Table 13: Showing differences in the average of the 7 mind-sets of OBCs in a B-School [Same sample at the beginning and at the end of Program]

	MS1	MS2	MS3	MS4	MS5	MS6	MS7
OBCs: Freshers							
[N: 70]	**72.6**	**86.4**	**59.4**	**52.8**	**33.0**	**66.0**	**46.2**
OBCs: End of Program							
[N: 70]	58.6	41.3	39.0	39.0	36.0	50.0	48.0

+++

The nature and dynamics of the 'trap-free mind' may be sensed by creative analysis of a beautiful **Zen parable** presented next.

TRY TO SEE the Zen parable from the vantage point of a Film Director. That 'seeing' involves creative projection. Reflection assisted by projection of the details represented by the words and sentences of the parable upon the 'inner dreaming screen'. It must be followed by analytic conceptualization of whatever observed in that 'seeing'.

The Master-Cook
Identity Crisis

Once upon a time in Japan, there was a great Samurai, named Kyozan. As he reached old age he started training young Samurais in his monastery. The Samurai community competed among themselves to enrol their children to be the disciples of Kyozan. He enjoyed the appreciation of the emperor and was often invited to the court as the head of a monastery.

Kyozan had a cook named Tosotsu.

The cook became fascinated with the art of swordplay of the Samurais.
The cook started nurturing a feeling that the art of sword is better than
the art of tea-ceremony in achieving wealth, recognition, and fame.
The fact of living with the greatest master and not able to learn his art
disturbed him.

Gradually, the cook decided to learn the art of sword from Kyozan.
But Kyozan accepted only the talented Samurais who had evidences
of competency in swordplay as disciples.

After months of sleepless conflicts, Tosotsu finally decided to learn the
art in secrecy. In hiding, he watched the Master's rituals, sessions with the
disciples, and spied the special guidance given to the parting disciples.
He could learn the techniques of the sword, the methods of practice, the
expressions and movements of a disciplined Samurai, ways of eating and
walking, the style of wearing the Samurai Kimono, and ways of talking.
He lifted a sword of the Master Samurai in order to practice the stolen
lessons. It was a sword gifted by the emperor, which the Master Samurai
had kept special but almost never used.

In a few years time, he realised that he had grasped even the deepest
secrets of sword when he witnessed a competition of the esteemed
Samurais of the Daimyos.

He earnestly longed for a way to test his learning.
By the next chance, he set out for a trip to the neighbouring province.
On the way he arranged the special Kimono of Samurais, wearing it he
walked along as an impeccable Samurai. Before he covered much distance
he could spot a Samurai. Observing his ways, Tosotsu approached him
and challenged for a duel. He could easily settle the opponent to ground.

Thereafter, the cook derived many more sojourns across the borders of
adjacent provinces. In the several episodes of confronting and challenging
Samurais, he did not undergo a single event of defeat.

+++

Tosotsu decided to part with his Master. He submitted the reason of settling down elsewhere as a peasant for the rest of his life.

IN the new location, nobody knew him. Happily he started living and moving around as a Samurai. Beyond a few months it was time for him to create an opportunity to demonstrate his prowess as a Samurai in the new location.

One day, he went to a local shrine where he saw an elderly Samurai amidst a humbled gathering. Tosotsu approached the spot and found him to be as agile as Kyozan. Without a second thought, Tosotsu announced his desire to have a duel.

The elderly Samurai gently replied that the duel could be held after fourteen days. Tosotsu had to agree to the condition. As he walked out, the entire gathering turned towards him. He overheard a few of them loudly wondering in a hushed voice:
     "This Samurai... challenged the Lightning Rose..!?"

It was a thunder in his innermost eyes. Tosotsu realised that the one he challenged was Shogen, a master swordsman of the country. He recalled Kyozan describing the special techniques of Shogen to the disciples, especially, about his magical sword known as 'Lightning Rose'.

As a fatally wounded warrior he wimped back to his hut. For the first time he felt shattered by the fear of death. He was swallowed by deep sorrow and remorse. By midnight he packed his things and set out back to the monastery of Kyozan to plead rejoining him as a cook.

When he reached the monastery, the Master Samurai was standing at the gate and welcomed him. Tosotsu could not hide his tears of guilt. He narrated his story from the conception of a desire to the death of it. By the end, Kyozan said:
     "The spirit of the sword does not die."

158

+++

Every night he practised with the old bamboo sword that he had made himself for initial days of practice. During the daytime he remained inside his cell and meditated on death.

On the day of his departure for the duel, the cook went to the room of Kyozan to bid farewell. The Master asked Tosotsu:

"What is the last act you want to do on this earth?"

"Cha-no-yu", the cook replied instantly.

Then the Master said:

"Then, take your cooking gears also.
Offer your last cup to the opponent."

"Yes, master."

At the arena, Shogen was amazed at the most brilliant Cha-no-yu he had ever seen. There was no tea maker. Only the tea.

The master warrior, whose first move would cut the sword of Tosotsu, gently accepted the tea from the hands of the opponent and said:

"You are a Master-Cook. I decide to spare your life."

Tosotsu bowed into deep silence...

Strategies to Escape the Mental TRAPS

The mental traps are to be resolved or transcended because of the following logic:

1. The mental TRAPS are not any original tendencies of the human entity. No other species seem to carry such traps.
2. With a trap-free mind any type and range of VUCA world of work, life, relationships can be journeyed without being defeated by tensions and feeling miserable and challenged again and again. The happiness purpose can be achieved by translating 'knowings' into elegant and complete 'doings' and desired 'states-of-being'.
3. The highest motives or drives of the spirit are about self-realization. The realisation required is about the nature of 'genius' or the attendant spirit inside, or the 'that' which is aware of whatever that it is aware of. The super-consciousness that sense the consciousness.
And such journeys become haywire carrying the load of the mental traps.

The mental traps can be resolved or transcended only 'indirectly'. Some primary strategies of transcending the mental traps are suggested.

1.
Try 'Variation'
Variation is the essence of the universe. Of the planet Earth and every slice of it. At the sub-atomic levels the particle varies itself into a wave and back to particle. And that interval itself varies [The 'Uncertainty Principle' of Werner Heisenberg]. All of that human creations, discoveries, inventions, modifications, and innovations are by 'variation' principle. All crafts, arts, dance forms, music forms, theatre, poetry, painting, and so on are by 'variations' of the available linkages. The very planet Earth is varying, the body is varying. A lyric is a variation of prose. Be a lyric with a beautiful tune. Instead of dry dull redundant prose.

A straight flute is generating magnificent curves of variations of its sounding. Of course, a genius is playing it. A straight line varies into alphabets and infinite type of hand-writing. Sound varies into music. Timing of sound varies into rhythms. BY the variation property of sounding: countless languages.

A vehicle climbing the heights of mountains has to vary several times its movements. Take the driver seat of the engines-of-intellect and vary the art and craft of your mind, your prose into lyrics, dialogues musical, and so on to climb the heights of your genius or attendant spirit.

So, a major strategy is to keep intently working on mental trap 6, namely rigidity and functional fixedness. 'Change' or 'shift' or apply 'variation' in existent ways of expressions, responses, behaviours, actions, work, dialogues, and relationships. Create 'evidences' of change. Do conscious 'duplication' of new and good expressions, responses, behaviours, actions, work, dialogues, and relationships observed in role models or personal heroes or deities and gods.

Manage to get good balance upon the bicycle of your attention
Especially, Attention-to-Details:
For instance, the term genius or its descriptions can be understood. There is no scope for attention-to-details contained in words and sentences. Instead, the real scope of 'details' are in the 'referent' or realities referred-to by the word, There is no scope for attention-to-details on the word 'glass'. But there is a lot of details hiding and enormous linkages to the 'reality' glass', the material glass.

Note that attention-to-details is increasingly disused because of the facilities, systems and setting of things and phenomena in the man-created environment. Usual normal life, work, relationship activities do not require even 10 percent of the engines of attention. The cats and birds are embodiments of attention - for their survival. But a genius individual is always in cool alertness to every detail around. Such attention-to-details define the core of a creative manager or genius leader.
The engine of attention shall not be strapped by the mental traps.

In order to try variation develop control over the engine of attention. Attention is the supreme engine of the entity - of all species too, including even plans and insects. Try gradually to balance it to pedal the way you want to in the terrain and the drive you decide. Attention creates and maintains the phenomenon in the internal world. For instance, take the case of illnesses. They are so real. But actually induced, developed, and reinforced by attention process only - at the core.

Severely mentally disordered people do not become ill despite serious anomalies in their body, lack of care and cleanliness, rotten food from the road, and so on. For, their attention is elsewhere. Train your attention every time to get out of trapping thoughts, feelings, sensations, illnesses, pains, worries, fears, anxieties, tensions, etc.

2.
Develop Creative Sensitivity
'Creative Sensitivity' is sensitivity that creates any new [new for the individual, may be present with everyone else] and high or varied orbits of linkages. The sensitivity that induces the fire and flight of inspiration. It involves the engines of attention-to-details, reflection, projection, conceptualization, trust in intuition, and the spirit of the will. By the desire to become great, become a cat of human being, to become a genius, to become self-realised. Try 'reflective reading' of great classics or the ones of choice. See that your physical movements and explorations are not delimited by the time-space-locations. Be eccentric in the inner laboratory and facilities.

Proceed to lonely journeys to wild forests or uninhabited areas. Observe birds, plants, tees, terrains, grass, flowers, stones, rivers, and so on. The human entity is at the core a 'creature of this planet' very much like a bird or fish or cat. It's sensitivities get triggered by exposure to nature processes. it may n it appeal to the logic of the 'person', the educated-intelligent self inside. SEE that human cat moving around with you, its great eyes, ears, and sensitivities of the deep engines of the mind, intellect, and attendant spirit.

BE A 'RE-SEARCHER'

Perhaps a fine 'state-of-being' is that of researcher-in-existence.
Researcher, not in any subject matters or technologies. Regardless of
the nature of the regular work you do search the entity and its sensing,
thinking, feeling, emotions, experiences, etc. The great laboratory of
life and self is always open, free. Do research to discover everything.
Including the orbit of super-consciousness.

Foremost clue: Search the known.
Is it ever possible to search the unknown? All the cues and clues to
the unknown are hidden in the known. The unknown itself cannot be
searched at all. The clues and cues about whatever unknown is present
in the known and available. No doubt about it.

Drive your sensitivity with the intentionality to 'create and-or to discover':

- Understand more and more about what you already know about
  you, not about what you do not know.
- Focus attention-to-details of your 'doing' - whatsoever be the
  doing. Because, every 'doing' is done for the benefit or use of
  some other|s. No doing is ultimately for one's own self or entity.
  Institutions, organizations, and even governments do not see this
  fact firmly and completely- that they are in existence for their
  domain of audience or beneficiaries or customers or clients.
  The voters and citizens. And, the new generation of children.
- Differentiate that a great manager or genius leader is first of all,
  a wonderful human being. Like a cat or rose. Be ready with an
  open mind. Corporate India needs wonderful creative managers
  and genius leaders.
- Always try something new, or challenging for you
  - like any music instrument, singing, painting, etc.
- Do experiments with your language in dialoguing as well as
  writing and in reading. Develop 'creative-language-control'.

Consider developing the following mind-sets:

- Don't belong to the degree and work experience you hold. You will become accordingly rigid. Take the decision to transcend the mental traps.
- Curiosity is the most critical requirement for creativity. [Everybody is creative because, everybody has that curiosity].
- But the curiosity to create the greater dimension of you. To create a strategy to transcend the mental traps. To do the self-analysis in a daring way. Curiosity about the very existence and to discover its great brilliance of wonder and simplicity. To get enlightened. To touch the gates to Satori. That taken-for-granted curiosity [used for mundane and centricity-conformity driven aspects] is actually driven by the 'original search response' of the child entity of human species, present in every other species by which they survive and sustain.

- Be clear about your questions. In creativity, questioning is very important. Try Socratic Questions. Read and reflect upon the parables of Zen. Live or 'do' the mind-sets of Jesus or Buddha, Krishna, Muhammad or whatever understood from the great mystics of the land or of other time-locations.
- Do sa creative self-analysis and get rid of self-importance and familiarity trap. See the you existing on the surface of planet Earth, rather than in a minor narrow space of the room or office or house. The human form itself is a trap only. Be beyond it. Then every plant, bird, and cat becomes sensible to the self. The seasons and winds, rivers and mountains become a part of your non-conscious. That is the state of poets and mystics, musicians and painters. Genius is precisely in that tuning. Not in awards and rewards, fame and wealth.
- See, re-see, re-read and creatively analyze great films, classics, and fiction. Try to see classical art-dance-music forms. Simply be interested in traversing the unusual track of interests and hobbies. Take leave and live alone for at least three days in a strange simple space-location.

- Buy a beautiful book and write your concepts-ideas. Not for anything. In fact, this very universe is actually a 'doing' not for anything that is logically acceptable to normal perceptions and knowing.
  Knowing it firmly is the beginning of a powerfully correct spiritual state-of-being.
- Try to see or develop an attitude or perspective that everyone who comes across you is lucky. Because, he or she or they have entered **your territory or space** of ongoing realities. Be alert for identifying evidences of greatness or wonder in everyone. Of course, in you too. If you disregard them then you become divisive. Someone is there because, they have come to 'YOU'. It is the way of your 'self respect', not 'self-importance'. People with self-importance must classify, divide, and separate others around, people [caste class creed role position, possessions, etc], events, entities, things, and phenomena. When you have that vantage-point you will be able to have creative interactions with them. That will enable your evolution and finally even Satori. Of course, that way you become the real 'creative manager' and 'genius leader'. Trainer or mystic guide.
- Develop a firm self trust. See the music director, dance director, and the film director. See their decision-firmness. Millions of monies are at stake.

Just DO NOT DOUBT whatever you are convinced about and accept and agree as truth. See the trust of the Cook to take the cooking gears to the Arena of Death. The logical traps drive a non-conscious seeking of evidences of a certain kind in order to trust 'firmly and completely'. SEE the kind of people who publicly declare God's blessing etc? Of course, the high performers and high achievers. As a result, the non-conscious analysis process would conclude that God is all about the glory and success, achievement and wealth; whereas, almost all known gods lived in pathetic tragedies.

The reality for you is the you. The setting of physical things, visible surroundings, activity or work, people, event, etc is the very first direct orbit of reality. The true referent reality linkages of the you.

The logic may prompt you to consider the grounding that there is reality beyond, to neighbourhoods, terrains, planet, solar system, and so on. Let it be. They are in real distant orbits from wherever your current positioning. But, that first orbit is your world.

The logic of scientific fact shall not trap you from being one with the existential reality. Practice creative analysis by using the variant-invariant-linkage-network-orbit-intentionality framework given in the book, 'The Missing Engines of Management Education' or 'Organizational Entelechy: Creative Manager, Genius Leader, Taoic process'; Prasad Sundararajan, Amazon.com

2

Reboot the mind and intellect: Instal new and sublime mind-sets:
Creating or developing altogether new mind-sets by choosing unique experience, reflective attention-to-details, doing meditation with the intent of escaping mental traps, interface with entities, things, and phenomena. Or by undergoing self-learning from great sources, training, mentoring, etc.

Understand the 'challenge and response' perspective of creativity and genius. Individuals are likely to feel incapable or unable and helpless that they cannot escape from the mental traps - such as the fear-tension-anxiety of the 'VUCA-world', strong drive for centricity-conformity, self-doubt and resource myopia, functional fixedness, sensitivity-lag, familiarity trap, self-importance, and speed.

Develop an 'I don't care' mind-set about self-doubt and resource myopia:
Of course, when other mental traps are managed, self-doubt and resource myopia would start vanishing like mist before the sun rays. It will reflect in your responses, behaviours, dialogues, etc. Because the efforts of getting out of mental traps are done 'consciously'. Whatever that gives confidence are to be expanded and evolved at elegant-complete-correct-taoic-firm level of expression or 'doing' and 'state-of-being'.

Seek feedback from a trusted friend or guide about the elegant-complete-correct, taoic-firmness of your 'doing' or 'knowing', so that you can trust them for creating the final picture of your being. Drive your sensitivity with the newly created gears of reading, extra activities, evolved aesthetics, etc.

Train your colleagues or spouse, or children to identify and analyse and transcend the mental traps. In fact, that is the best way to transcend your own mental traps. Train the children to be grateful to the teachers. To look at them from the vantage point of 'guru' whatsoever their identities are. Children love and regard their parents regardless of their identities. Then why not teachers too? *Matha-Pitha-Guro Daivam.* Modern generation does not have that sense of genuine gratitude to teachers to whom they were listening to for average 13 years continuously. Much more than they looked at the face of anyone else in their life.

The teachers are a great victim of familiarity trap and self-importance trap. The term teacher is very mechanical. Not conducive to the development of inspired learning in students. If the students are really remote from somebody known to them, it is the teachers. Needles to say, they have simply duplicated that mind-set of distance from the very modern teachers only who contribute nothing else to students than lessons for rote-learning and writing examinations.

3
Resolve the 'Core' of Fear-Tension-Anxiety
Try directly to understand the referred-to reality of the so-called fear, tension, and anxiety. Verify that there is the mind-sets of self importance driving the fear. Just don't try to control or repress or escape from fear. But direct attention to the origin of fear somewhere inside. It is actually, the 'fear of death'. Everything in the universe would vary and vanish. Not that only you die. The very planet will cease to exist in this way after tens of thousands of years. Nothing is beyond death.

See the 'creature', its flesh-blood-bone body, organs and glands, central nervous system, abdomen, hands, etc. The 'creature' is NOT afraid.

Search the internal space like a master-thief for the precise time, space, and location of that spy. Steal it out of that zone and throw away among the stalk of cheap documents.

As a strategy to escape the fear and anxiety of failure, one can try new responses and behaviours and actions, altogether new readings, new side work of various kinds available, new complex relationships with the competent people or activities and getting ready to be a failure, to be ridiculed by others. Try new things and be friendly with failures.

Analyse that feeling of failure. Understand eccentricity.
Develop controlled eccentricities in tour eating, sleeping, walking, responses, behaviours, actions, relationships, and especially dialogues. Try some new musical instruments; or writing poetry, doing painting, and so on. Buy new books and do Book Review. Respond to the book. Write a book review of 'Illusions' by Richard Bach. Just for the sake of it. For your child or friend or spouse to read. Or for you to read after three years. Try reading new subjects, especially philosophies, new activities and when you are in contact with some eccentric people, do some dance, do some music, do some theatre and so on.

Create a new 'fearless-self' by your own internal dialoguing and negotiating with the existent you and represent that new identity.
Like the mystics, sages, saints do. It must work some what like the 'designations' work for you [if..!?]. To create a great identity, you need to use the force of intercourse with your own internal dialogue. To impregnate your 'doing' with supreme firmness and completeness and elegance, good flow and correctness.

You need to develop responses-behaviors-actions-dialogues that are in Tao [harmonious flow] with the new identity. For instance, if the new or required identity is that of a prince or princess, leader or manager, teacher or doctor, researcher or administrator, man woman, husband wife, etc, you need to have an identity designed for taking that role and 'doing' the linkaged functions and activities. Realise: all conflicts - external and internal - are due to mental traps.

4
Develop a 'Universe-Perspective' about You.
If any tension - see the planet earth. Develop a hero's mind-set or heroic mind-set. Mind-sets of greatness as you see and understand in history, stories, fictions, fairy tales, myths, parables, and even movies of great successes. Despite whatsoever trials and tribulations, threats and dangers, attacks and humiliations and intimidations of all kinds. Or develop other greater mind-settings of real life heroes or of your own deities.

And somehow get out of centricity-conformity mind-settings. About food, sexuality, social status, etc or at least that which you consider not okay with you. Try to see the feminine wonder in every woman, get out of the jails of looking at a female from the vantage-points of the male centricity-conformity. Respect every female. Respect every one.

Perhaps this perspective is applicable to the very females also. All human entities are carried by the womb of the woman and the primal food from her breast. Mothers are to get closer to their genius to become eligible to be worshipped by their children. That cannot happen by the designations, money, and possessiveness.

Try identifying the variant-invariant linkage-network-orbits of you and your existence. If the very God comes before the individual creature and its engines have to work to render a perception of it. And that perception occurs where? In the very consciousness driven by the engines of the body, which finally again god's own creation with god's own material 100 percent..! How come you straight subscribe to some externalized definitions, descriptions, explanations and interpretations about the very you? You may use the mind-sets of 'knowings', but verify them vis-à-vis your direct experience and reflective analytical conclusions.

Try to see the process reality and the 'continuity principle' of your consciousness and body processes, as well as of the universe and planet Earth and existence in all its details. ['Continuity Principle' is given in the book: Missing engines of management education, Prasad Sundararajan, Amazon.com].

5

Develop the 'Creature Perspective' [given in the book: 'Missing engines of management education']. Identify how mind-sets are working like 'conditioned response of dog's salivation' in a Pavlovian experiment. Conditioned salivations of your trapping mind-sets, dialogues, responses, behaviors, and actions. Details of 'creature perspective' are given in the book 'Organization Entelechy: Creative manager, Genius Leader, Taoic Process' [Amazon.com].

See the tip of the universe operating in the design-setting-process of your 'creature'. Reflect upon your identity. Where were you before the age of three years? What kind of you if you were born in a different time-space-location?

See the simple gentle infant that you were once upon a time. How come you have all these mind-sets and mind-settings. See the transience of all the mind-settings. Accept that they are all for the so-named survival and sustenance. Understand the drama of life and the 'theatre' or drama that runs through the mindberg vis-à-vis life-work-relationships.

6

Develop the 'Film Director's Perspective':
In our research, the Film Directors are found to be of a high scale of creativity and originality. Simply because, a film did not exist before its occurrence. Direct your expressions, responses, actions, dialogues, work, and relationships wit tao and elegance.

Be the producer, director, setting designer, script writer, actor, and even the audience - all in you. Great Film Directors are least bothered about their own fame and publicity. They just do what they are most creative and original.

Identify events and actions that you have done sometime in your life and analyze them as a creative case studies and derive conclusions and creative feedback about the magic and wonder of you.

7
Develop creative-language-control
Language is finally, the only one method for you to train yourself.
Apply creative attention, reflection, and pause in reading, listening,
talking, thinking, and dialoguing. Language is just a statistical tool
of communication or conveying messages and reports about mental
impressions, knowings, etc about observed realities. Language in itself
has no reality. It does not exist anywhere else than in the minds and
exchange of people. Not even in the printed books and recorded devices.
Reflect upon it. The language is not 'written' anywhere in the body.
Reflect upon it and see the linkages.

On one side, language sensitizes you to the referred-to realities. Language
is supremely powerful also. Use it to inspire you, refine you, as a tool to
discover or search truth, as a method to guide your attention to access
self-realization or Satori. Creative language control is about control on
sensing the reality using it as a tool or method. The mental traps operate
like sort of languages inside. Develop the engine of language instead of
taking it for granted as the most familiar doing. With that kind of
power of creative language, manage the mental traps.

8
Analyze and resolve 'Self-importance Trap'
SEE: When the mental trap of self-importance becomes high and extreme
- coupled with rigidity, sensitivity-lag, fear-tension-anxiety of failure, loss
fear-and-anxiety of low-ness – then: the evils, or evil minds, traitors and
such rage scale criminals who are after control and power over people,
obsessed about security, safety, etc. The evil knows well the details of evil.
But they are victims of some desire or greed driven by severe
mental traps.

Give permission to your consciousness to love-respect your ongoing self.
And thereby get rid of the trap of 'Self-Importance'. The others especially
in India would consider, respect or show 'importance' only to hose
with highness in money, wealth, power, high-caste-class, etc. It is an
'importance factor'. Not genuine 'respect factor' that works behind.

So you crave to capture linkages of societal importance. Importance in your social-network, in your family, with your friends, with the reference groups in the location or at national and global levels.

Instead, just maintain self-respect fully realising how you keep and maintain a respected thing inside your house. The need for self-importance is linkaged to the importance of espoused values, beliefs, norms, ideologies also. For example, some think that their God or belief is the greatest whereas others think their's is the greatest.

This resulted in conflicts and wars, homicides and genocides.

Individuals tend to carry so much of self-importance in maintaining their stances, opinions, attitudes, beliefs, perspectives, etc. Human beings are capable of evaluating even the god and deities and related history and ideologies. One god or one ideology or one knowing is greater or more important than the others. If the god is 'loved unconditionally', then it may lead to better state of consciousness than the perspective of 'god is love'.

The foundations of the genius, of the good and the right and the elegant, are inside, not outside. Just build the required scaffolding to create a you of your design and setting. Poornam must arise out of poornam.

By self-respect the first step towards poornam is accessed.

Respect all your knowings, doings, and states-of-being. Respect your responses, actions, behaviours, dialogues, work, and relationships.

9

Transcend the Familiarity | Taken-for-Granted Attitude Trap

The clear existence of such a mental trap has been differentiated during the decades-long research on creativity, originality, genius, and related human entelechies. The expressions, responses, behaviors, actions, and dialogues of the thousands of participants during the 1-2-3 days workshops on mind-sets, provided clear evidences to conceptualize such a mental trap. It has been clearly observed that Familiarity Trap intervene the [1] expressions, [2] responses, [3] behaviors, [4] actions, [5] dialogues, [6] work, and [7] relationships of people. You too can discern familiarity trap in these aspects with the very you.

172

In a way, the familiarity trap is really vicious. It generates the 'taken-for-granted attitude to everything familiar. And, the modern high-tech communication systems, visual-media, internet, etc have made the entire world of things, entities, phenomena, people, etc very 'familiar'. The 'mystery' of existence, the world, the universe, is lost. Even the so-called God is not a mystery. Attention to the existence of things is waiting for they becoming 'endangered'.

This lack of 'mystery' induces sort of numbness to the processes of the very mind and intellect, and thereby of the spirit,

- Reflect and introspect. See the variant-invariant-orbit -linkage-intent-network of existence.
- Create self-sustainable self-image instead of continuing with duplicated internal dialogues of self-importance and get rid of familiarity-trap.
- Have a Zen mind***: read-reflect-think about the messages in the classic treatises of Zen. Reflect upon some parables of Zen.
- Redefine your self-image as a genius or creative individual.
- Be always aware that the social-network or people around in India are centricity-conformity driven to criticize you and humiliate you. Despite shivering heart, climb the Everest. Escape the complex rooms of the palace where the soldiers are waiting to catch you.
- Just never take the work for granted. There could be severe depressions about the lost hopes, desired positions never achieved etc. But, the given reality is the given work. The tree of your work happened to be there. So be there firmly, correctly, elegantly, in good flow, and completely. Till the moment you vacate. It is the logic for the work of living also.
- Just never take the spouse for granted. The tree happens to be there till the moment of departure signal. Of whatever kind.

***Living by Zen you 'serve humanity humbly, fulfilling your presence in this world with loving kindness and observing your passing as a petal falling from a flower' [Paul Reps and Nyogen Senzaki, 1994]

Orbit 2 Strategies: More Subtle

1
Manage the Speed Trap:
Just do not expect or anticipate quick results. Manage the state of 'hurry'.
Develop high scale of 'patience'. Be cool about existence. Get out of the
emotions of 'fear, tension, and anxiety' resulting from comparison of all
kinds. Be the 'Master Samurai'. Have the patience of the master of the
Lightning Rose. Be aware of the fact that the mind and intellect
become infected by the speed trap.

Develop clarity:
- realise how to speed up, when to speed up, where to speed up
- identify: why do you want speed?
- even in clear highways, sometimes drive really slow..!

See that any event or act, expression, and responses of you when you do
the so-called 'puja'. Maintain impeccable cat-like attention-to-details. Be
slow. You splash water, set flowers, trigger incense, and then inspire the
flame. That is the design setting of your act. Let it be a cha-no-yu.
- What are the details of that act of your puja or 'Cha-No-Yu'?
- What is the process inside your mind, intellect, spirit?
- Who or more precisely, 'what' is on the 'other side'?

When you change your understanding about a thing, it will change.
If that thing is in trouble or in damaged 'state-of-being', you can repair
that thing provided you know how to do it [and provided you sense the
beginnings of the problem, also]. So too with a phenomenon, event, or
with forming of a form, book, designing things, etc.

When you understand a human being, and give feedback, that non-
conscious mindberg changes to that extent. That should be the nature and
power of your understanding, drawing his or her unique strengths, seeing
the invisible linkages of his or her Double. When you do it in responses-
behaviors-actions-dialogues and work then you certainly become a
genius-leader.

When the mental traps are understood and resolved, you become the embodiment of the Zen Mind. You tend towards powers of a Master Samurai in whatever your activities, and blessed with several Satories of new concepts, ideas, and perspectives.

2
Be aware of the basic evidences about the Mind:
- Mind is primary: The first engine to develop fully, even in the womb
- Mind carries primacy: The most-dominating engine
- Mind is analytical [by linkage-network with the engines-of-intellect]
- Mind is emotive: direct linkages with all engines of emotions-feelings
- **Mind is process and product at the same time**

Mind is that which you are aware of - RIGHT NOW. Whatever that is aware of the mind is sort of super-consciousness around you. It is actually simple, but the entire philosophies, mysticism, and the subject of Psychology are about the mind. It is all the time with you. Try to sense it with confidence, free mind, and will. And induced in children, is the concept of God or Almighty with the hope of he or she differentiating it one day. You were exposed to ideas of spirituality, so that one day you will open the gateless-gate of Satori.

Develop trap-free mid with the intention of creating and maintaining a peaceful, harmonious, and ethical you capable of discerning good, right, correct from bad, wrong, incorrect. Reflect for sometime, how they got contaminated with fears and anxieties to such an extent that they became 'trapping mind-sets'. Or why those required blocks or controls and regulations of expressions have to work trapping you from achieving the same goals and purposes?

For instance: See what generally happens to the growing-developing human entities during early years in great frequency and reinforcements.

Try to avoid too much of occurrences of the following nature in your training and guiding of children or colleagues, others, etc.

- Copying the fear and anxiety from others about uncertain, new, vague, strange, eccentric, etc kind of situations, people, ideas, events, entities, things, and phenomena.
- Copying fear an anxiety about failure, uncertain future.
- Developing fear and anxiety about humiliation and ostracization, low-ness and inferiorities.
- Becoming myopic about resources, developing self-doubt.
- Carefully avoid the languages that may induce mental traps.
- Duplicating, copying, learning rigidity in thought and responses, behaviours, and actions.
- Development of self-importance. Instead train him or her to differentiate self-respect.
- To be alert about speed trap and familiarity traps.

Expose the inner film to the nature-processes and its entities, things, and phenomena; higher or greater expressions of responses, behaviours, actions, and dialogues – such as in films, dance and music; or to great concepts-ideas-perspectives and thereby capable of detachment from 'familiarity trap' and self-importance traps.

3
LIVE YOUR NAME: IF IT IS A GOOD WORD, USE IT AS YOUR KEY-WORD

To create a greater dimension of you by analysing the linkages and orbits of the referent reality of that 'key-word'. That is, SEE the referent of the word that names you. See its realities, linkages, orbits. If required, create a great name to reflect the evolved you. The Rishis and Mystics of all traditions have renamed themselves or other re-named them.

The existent name symbolises the duplicated, copied, enforced contents and mind-sets, including the mental traps. Change your signature by graphological entelechy. Yet, try setting the purpose in life as to finally identify that nameless 'being'.

In a way, the designation - the role 'name' too can work the same way. See the engines required for a manager or leader worth the name. Write your existent or new name on a beautiful notebook that invites you to write something in it. Write your own notes about significant ideas, perceptions, feelings, thoughts, experiences, interactions, etc with a free-wheeling mind and intellect. Maintain Creative Language-Control in the process of writing and talking. Make the writing or talking better or more creative everyday. Take time from internet to do the interactions with the bicycle of your own silent genius inside.

See, there must be the 'creative force'. Then only the orgasmic Satori. Similar creative energy is to be applied to the engines-of-intellect. Best by great readings. A great blessing of travelling through the incubative mind-intellect-spirit of great researchers, philosophers, mystics.

'Think as you read and read as you think' – Chinese proverb. Every new concept-idea is a new room, new energy field, new scaffolding, new expansion of the cortical regions of the brain.

Re-read and analyse the concepts in books such as:
The Dancing Wu-Li Masters, The Story of Philosophy,
Zen flesh and Zen Bones, Tao Te Ching, I Ching,
The Turning Point, Jonathan Livingston Seagull, Illusions,
The Master-Thief: Stealing sources inside,The Tao of Physics,
Tao: the Watercourse, Missing Engines of Management Education
Organization Entelechy: Creative Manager, Genius Leader,
Taoic Process
At least three of the Core Upanishads, Gitanjali, Zorba the Greek,
The Don Flows Quiet, Zen and the Japanese Culture

Escape like a cat of the Master Thief out of the mental trap of fear, tension, and anxiety of humiliation, low-ness, inferiority-feeling etc by:

- 'doing' actions or acts that the others around are likely to observe for its beauty and elegance and uniqueness

- trying different make up, hair style, grow beard if not a practice, wear unique or different good dresses, get into different type of social-networks, join clubs of sports and games, etc.
- resolving inferiorities if any, straight face it reflect about them and switch them off
- 'doing' some singing, or dancing, diary writing, or great readings
- developing 'controlled eccentricity'.

Certain degree of eccentricity can definitely help escape from the traps of worries and disillusionment and ambiguity in life-work-relationships. The best way is to change the way you talk by adding certain pause in between, changing pitch, speed, and volume - as in theatre or films. If required, correcting words and sentences for including a trace of higher planes of whatever discussed.

Don't feel embarrassed to talk philosophy. Do not feel 'low' and surrender to critiques. But try to be a mystic philosopher in your dialogues and ways of life, work, relationships. The highest university degree offered is called 'Doctor of Philosophy', whatsoever sciences and technologies and anti-philosophical the subject matter researched.

Be certain that India is a land of mystics, philosophers, Rishis and their Vedas and Vedantas, Upanishads and Gita. Develop good reading in one or more of them. The Are simply sublimely great. See that most of those who carry the fear-and-anxiety of 'criticism' or 'low-ness' and inferiority-feeling about being philosophical go and surrender to a guru for ensuring the path of happiness or to deities in the temples and do ritualistic marriage and so on! India is a land where those who live by their philosophy including of so-called Gandhian one, are viewed with sort of 'positive disdain' as great majority of them are likely to be in the 'lower' class or communities, low in especially the economic or richness hierarchy. Everyone feels great inside. But no courage and confidence to manifest it outside. Great romantic ideas and visualisations inside. But emptiness and apathetic outside. As if those things are to be kept saved in lockers to be submitted somewhere else after death.

Beware of the usual internal chatting: 'free-floating thoughts'. Just direct your film-of-existence. Don't worry about the audience. Just don't add 'masalas' only to trap audience. Be a Director with the theatre of life outside and inside. Be original as the Director of your live film.

Do think, but don't get worried about the contents of thoughts if they carry linkages of worry and failure and relationship conflicts. Don't get trapped by the emotive linkages of those thoughts, even if they are about the real and expected. Because, thought are thoughts are thoughts only. No direct wiring with any referent-reality. All thoughts are sort of imagination. Even if it is about the truth. Even if they are about the pain directly felt on the hands. Take clues from these kind of ideas in this book and make your interpretations and analysis in your beautiful project diary. **Just take the next step.** Like Edmund Hillary said: 'At 3,000 feet height on the mighty Everest, my heart was trembling with fear. Yet, I continued climbing'. So, start climbing the next step.

Design and develop a clear 'identity'.
Then any disturbing aspects of personal history, 'lowness' of ongoing life-work-relationships, worries about lost hopes, damaged desires, etc cannot shake you. See whether there are elements of greed, jealousy, envy, etc in the details of that 'identity'. Let the new identity be as strong and sublime as you can design. You may get ample clues from the book, 'The Master Thief: Stealing Resources inside', Prasad Sundararajan, Amazon.com

Develop inspiration for 'creative dialoguing' with colleagues or friends, instead of small talks and time-pass conversations on ordinary-usual topics.

Discover a Creative Genuine Mentor.
Who is a real powerful Mentor or Trainer? He or she must be like a Music Director or Film Director. The one who refines the prose of you into lyrics, render a beautiful tune to it, and make you sing it. If you are a lyric, you will come across a tuned life. A real mentor will 'film-direct' your responses, behaviours, actions, work, dialogues, relationships. The real trainer or mentor will provide you 'creative feedback'. A feedback that helps creating a greater orbit of your self, mind, intellect.

See the truth: 'the path of life depends upon the level of your preparation'. Prepare you to be unique or great. Then the unique and great path will appear before you. No doubt.

4
Yoga and Mental Traps

Take the simplest truth. Whatever you 'sense' about you, [whatever you refer-to by that word 'you' or 'me' or 'I' - and the expanse to which your consciousness or attention goes to capture that domain of the you], as the you. As the only you. Nothing more than that. Why do you subject your sensing of you taken-for-granted? Just because, it is all the time there. IN fact, yoga is a general term to denote your tuning or becoming one with that entity with you, carrying you since embryonic times.

Simple lonely walking is good. If possible, through 'natural terrains'. Walking is an activity where both the sides of the brain becomes active. The right side coordinating the left side and the vice versa.
Focus attention on the abdominal region. Try to discern that super-consciousness that is maintaining absolute continuity in awareness about whatever in the consciousness or mind or body. See the orbits of the non-conscious, then conscious, and then the super-conscious that covers every linkage in the n-dimensional flow of things around and within. These are all just clues. Get the invariant of the clues. Every step of yoga is like 'illogical dots'. They will get linkaged later. From that point onwards it is absolute balance of mind. State of 'genius-being'

☺ Out of all, practice 'soorya-namaskaram': Especially in todays salient ways of sedentary life, 'sooryanamaskaram' is perhaps the most critically significant procedure that works on the critical junctions of the physical body [which gets the most blocked in sedentary styles of life]. Perhaps every bird and cat and dog does 'soorya-namaskaram' sort of bodily actions. Develop attention on the super-consciousness by treating the body as a separate entity doing the movements and postures. Metaphorically, the body is the bicycle and the you the one who pedals it, and the super-consciousness being aware of both.

As a supplement, 'shavasanam' also should be practised. The purpose is to achieve fine linkages with the near-complete state of relaxation to the body.

To achieve the state of the body of a one year old child in sleep. Dare to reflect upon fear, or tension, or anxiety, especially of death during 'shavasana'. Incubate and differentiate the three core situations of survival-sustenance: choice, decision, and action. Then verify the 'state-of-being' of oneself.

Pranayama: Pranayama, is exercising the ultimate engine of respiration. Moreover, respiration is directly linkaged with 'talking' or sounding, and 'thinking' [thoughts are un-uttered sounding]. So balance on the bicycle of respiration will render greater dimensions of mastery over the engines of intellect, especially thinking [other organic consequences also].

Do pranayama correctly, elegantly, and completely. With your 'sanyamic' attention ['sanyamic': patient alertness + reflection + sensitivity]. Constantly carefully drive your attention to find out not the 'what' in you is 'doing' the act of respiration. In the given design-setting-process, the creature does it. Take it is a 'doing' managed by the Double of the creature. For instance, when you run or feel tense the respiration increases or decreases. Therefore, when you take or access control over that ultimate engine of the creature, that much of your consciousness become attuned with that 'original doing' of the creature. Use the bicycle metaphor. But in case of prana-ayama or exercising of the movements of the very basic energy or prana into the body, see the 'you' on one pedal and try to locate the 'that' which is doing the other pedal.

+++
By observing another dancer, only the external movement can be duplicated. the internal engines that drive it are absolutely invisible even if described. Increasingly challenging, if the dance you want to learn is one of a higher style and dimension. Whatever dance externally visible is because of the dancer 'following something else that guides the dance'. In case of dance it is the three spoked wheel of lyric, tune, and rhythm.

181

Those movements you see of a master or a model is possible only because of their tuning with the music and rhythm. SO, if you really want to master the dance, then follow the lyric-music-rhythm. Do not try duplicating, imitating, approximating the external movements of the dance. This is the truth about every dance. The 'doing' of every dance.

5
Mental Trap Resolution by Mind-set Analysis Workshops and Individual Training Programs

As mentioned earlier, clear awareness about the details of mental traps and the extent of their presence or absence in oneself does wonders. Evidenced in every training program or workshops. Because, the 'feedback' creates all learning. Mind-set Analysis induce clarity about traps + provides 'creative feedback'. Sensitization to the pattern and extent of mental traps has been found to be significantly effective in helping the participants to develop clues to resolve their mental traps. Whenever the PNK-Questionnaire was administered, 'before' the workshop procedure and by the end of the third month, a significant reduction in the extent of mental traps and shift in pattern was found every time. A sample of such differences assessed for a group of senior managers [N: 25] is presented below.

Table 14: PNK-Questionnaire Scores Before Training and After Training
Sample N: 23

Before Training

Mental Traps	MS1	MS2	MS3	MS4	MS5	MS6	MS7
Mean	44.76	41.32	35.90	31.00	26.00	41.03	38.90
SD	15.70	17.50	9.10	12.70	14.60	13.60	11.70

After Training

	MS1	MS2	MS3	MS4	MS5	MS6	MS7
Mean	33.90	28.70	27.80	17.00	14.10	31.30	28.40
SD	17.00	16.20	12.80	10.00	6.80	15.20	12.70

Difference in mind-set scores

	MS1	MS2	MS3	MS4	MS5	MS6	MS7
Before-After	10.86	12.62	8.10	14.00	11.90	9.73	10.50

The Logic of 'Generalizing' the findings to 'Corporate India'

All creations and discoveries are based on expanding and interpreting the linkages of the available.

Why the findings from 5,050 [13,365 respondents are generalized to the whole of 'Corporate India'-?

The evidences based on a miniscule sample [though supplemented by a larger sample of 13,365] can be generalised to the reality of Corporate India by virtue of the following facts:

[1] The data is on 'mind-sets'. Not on abilities or personality factors. The core processes of the mindberg of human beings must be more-or-less identical, such as the processes of the body, intelligence, intellect, and spirit.

The basic nature and dynamics of the mindberg must be more or less similar to the whole of species. In other words, even if the entire population of corporate personnel responds to the PNK-Questionnaire, the average would not show any significant differences. Of course, unless and until the mind-sets are shifted by systematic procedures or by sheer coincidence of unique shift experiences..

The data reported, of course, has been relevant only for the sample of 5,050 respondents. They were all either participants in 2-3 days training workshop or minimum 3-hour seminars on mental 'blocks-traps'. Whoever present in such setting might have developed insights on shifts in perspective and self-image. The only difference is that the entire population of India did not do the PNK-Questionnaire. Even if, the results are unlikely to be much different from whatever reported in this work.

[2] The mental traps are linkaged with the primary or by-birth emotive states of fear-tension-anxiety.
All he mental traps including rigidity, sensitivity-lag, familiarity trap, and self-importance are directly linkaged with fear and anxiety; the basic emotions programmed as a protective force to every entity.

[3] The basic mind-sets that become mental traps are essential for survival sustenance and social adaptation. Therefore, they must be present at least as threshold mental 'blocks' in every human being, wherever.

And, the mental traps are easily possible expansions and extensions of such basic mind-sets. The Indian environment of parenting, schooling, administrative-service-commerce processes, media, traditions, myths, stories, literature, film etc are filled with cues for triggering and reinforcing the mental 'blocks' to develop into mental 'traps'.

Thus, once again, the Core Logic of Generalization as follows:

First of all, the nature and basic emotive processes of the 'mind' must be of comparable levels for a larger population.

Second of all, the environment of incessant small talks and informal communication whenever and wherever people meet must be of similar pattern in a social, cultural, historical location; the myths, aesthetics, traditions, norms, folkways, practices, rituals, etc of socialization, and so on must be of common ground linkages in determining expressions, responses, behaviours, actions, work, relationships, and dialogue patterns.

Third of all, the media contents – newspaper, TV serials, films, carry messages and news that unambiguously provide ample evidences of mental traps. Only critical difference is that the anomalies and manifestations of the kind have never ben looked at from the vantage-point of mental traps.

Finally, the data across varied samples do not show any significant variations or differences. The number of individuals with 'low' scores is so low in number [a mere 87 out of 5,050 participants]. That implies the more-or-less uniform level of mental 'traps' with the general population. In other words, even if the whole of educated India responds to the questionnaire, the 'mean' or pattern of medium-high' mental traps will be the same as those of the great majority of the remaining 13,365 respondents in this study.

Therefore, the findings can be generalized to indicate the possible-probable state of mental traps in Corporate India and the genius-loci of the very nation ...

+++
Note:
By reflective reading and conceptualization write down your own observations, analysis, conclusions, and recommendations.

+++
SPECIAL NOTE:
If you want to know the extent of mental traps in you, fill the questionnaire and send the responses to email: geniusachoice@gmail.com and verify your mental trap pattern. If it is 'low' you are one of the 6 percent of individuals with a 'trap-free mind and intellect' denoting clear **potentiality** for the entelechy of creativity, originality, and genius. If not, this book is to be subjected to your creative-analytical reading, at least.

If your scores are medium to high, then the feedback will carry individual specific strategies for managing resolution and transcendence of mental traps. If your scores are low, then, you are definitely a potentially creative, or original, or genius individual. Knowing that can work as an inspiration to seek guidance and creative feedback from a competent trainer or mentor.

The Core Observations, Conclusions, and Recommendations

Summary of the grounding of this book:

1

The concept of mental trap [also called 'Psychological Trap'] refers to certain 'non-conscious or unconscious mind-sets' that block the creative and original functions of the mind, intellect, and spirit of human beings. This book is about 9 core mental traps. At their core is 'fear and anxiety'. All of them carry the power to block the entelechy possible-probable for the human being. Everyone of them tend to interfere with the quality and completeness of the expressions, responses, behaviors, actions, dialogues; self, work, and relationships of individuals. And, it must be noted that the mental traps block sensitivity to the very mental traps.

2

The data on mind-sets has been collected during one-day seminars or 2-3-5 day workshops, and class-room sessions on the themes of creative-analytic-thinking, creative management, genius leadership, creative ethics, mind-set analysis, etc.

3

At least 4,500+ managers at all levels and B-School students were observed from the 'researcher's vantage-point' ['participant observation'-a method in behavioral-social sciences] during training workshops and class-room sessions.

Observations and Conclusions

[1]
Mental 'traps' are a majority-phenomena in Corporate India.

Out of the sample of 5,050 consisting of administrators, managers, and management students [the primary sample representing 'corporate India'], about 1,945 respondents revealed relatively 'low' mental traps which indicates a state relatively closer to a trap-free mind-setting entailing creativity in work, behaviours, and relationship management. The remaining 61 per cent showed 'medium -to- high' mental traps. Not conducive to creative or great performance and thereby the entelechy of institutions, organizations, governance become liable to be decelerated and-or retarded.

However, 87 respondents [out of 1,945] revealed freedom from mental traps showing only the minimal or essential threshold mental 'blocks'. And, all of them presented evidences of creativity and originality, greater 'self-image', high and varied competencies, record of recognitions, special achievements in their workplaces, happy and smart, self-satisfied, well-balanced in mind-intellect, and life-work-relationships, and so on. So, a trap-free mind is a great achievement.

The finding could be generalized to 'Corporate India'
On the basis of the following observations:

- The respondents were from Indian institutions and organizations of varied types, across sectors, and scales of operations.
- The average scores of mental traps of the larger sample [N: 13,365] are used as a reference point. The similarity with the mental traps of the larger sample indicates the feasibility of generalization.
- The extent and pattern of mental traps showed no significant variation vis-à-vis levels of education, job positions, and work experience within the primary sample of 5,050 as well as in the general sample of 13,365 respondents.

[2]
**High mental traps clearly block self-perception and
awareness about the quality of 'doing' and 'being'.**

The highly educated and employed people did not seem to be
aware of any mental blocks or traps in the beginning of the workshops.
Most of them were unaware of the fact that their expressions, responses,
behaviours, actions, and dialogues, and learnt activities are more or less
directly governed by the non-conscious mind-sets. They had no idea that
many of their past initiatives and inspirations were disregarded because of
mental traps and intellect-traps. They did not know that their genius was
blocked only by mental traps. That their job performance, or quality of
responses, behaviours, actions, and managing of relationships could have
been much wonderful or great and creative, with a trap-free mind-setting.
It is a fact: 'knowing' does not directly entail the 'doing' and 'being'
[of the 'knowing'].

In the beginning of training programs and Mind-set Analysis Workshops,
the respondents with 'medium-high-severe' mental traps manifested the
following general behaviours:

- 'no-question and no-response' mode despite the ambience of
  free-wheeling of ideas and discussions ['to talk' foolish -
  duplicating the idea of Steve Jobs],
- appeared irritated about the lack of 'logical' structure and lack
  of ppts and a linear logic for the workshop, despite explanations
  using the metaphor of 'strange dots getting connected at the end'
  as in a film; they could not tolerate the ambiguity of strange dots
  that may get connected later,
- showed no significant interest in 'creative-analytic perception'
  [reading between the lines and seeing the unreported or
  unspoken, looking at a thing, event, idea, from different
  vantage-points, etc] of a brilliant Zen parable,
- not-doing the assignments; showing expressions, responses,
  behaviours, actions, and dialogues of familiarity trap and
  self-importance.

From that inertia, they shifted their attention to more details towards the end of the workshops or class sessions. **Almost everyone** manifested better quality and quantity of responses. In few cases magical shifts could be observed with those who did more genuine introspection and self-analysis of their mental traps.

Those few with 'threshold' scores and 'low' scores in mental traps were found to be open-minded and spontaneous in expressions, in responses, behaviours, and dialogues; and inspired about 'creative-analysis' of the parables given as case studies***.

*** Usually, only one [in a group of average 15 participants] would score relatively 'lower' mental traps. The remaining would be of 'medium' and 'high' scores by the mind-set Questionnaire. As a norm of such workshops, those with the lowest scores would be asked to explain "why his or her scores are low..!" Invariably, 'low-scorers' [87 out of 5,050] narrated an exceptional, or creative, or special story of early development and-or about unique-special activities, interests, plus a clear purpose and philosophy in life or work.

Such an open description of unique personal history was publicly asked for due to certain creative logic, mentioned below:

- **First of all**: to prove the validity of the PNK-questionnaire by eliciting 'evidences' from individuals on the spot [low-scorers revealing their unique stories that corroborated their 'freedom from mental traps'].
- **Second of all:** to provide evidence to the others present that unique, special, creative-original expressions, responses, behaviours, actions, work, dialogues, and relationships are possible only with the facility of the free-wheeling engines of the mind-intellect-spirit.
- **Third of all:** to trigger the inspiration of other participants [who scored 'medium-High' mental traps] to take a shift in perspective and self-image as well as to work out strategies for developing 'trap-free' minds.

+++

Of course, all kinds of great things are blocked or concealed
from easy access. Whether man-created or nature-created
or God-created. That is why, one has to 'steal' one's own
resources or great engine-powers like a Master-Thief
steals the most precious jewel from the central most
room of a highly fortified palace of a powerful feudal chief.

+++

If the great and powerful engines of the entity start working or operating
on their own choice, then the person will go mad and die. Therefore, the
design-setting-processs is such that they develop, evolve, and function
only according to the level of learning and practising and intent.

[3]
From the vantage point of the findings of this data, it seems that the culture and climate of creativity and genius is blocked in Corporate India and therefore, in India.

It is of unique significance that the extent and pattern of the mental traps
of the primary sample of 5,050 is not much different from the larger
sample of population who are not leaders or managers or administrators.

IF a critical mass of managers and administrators are sensitized to the
entelechies of their 'trap-free' minds and intellects, they can certainly
impact the choices, decisions, and actions that must elevate Corporate
India towards top-class performance. They will invariably discover their
engine-powers and enlightenments and even Satori subsequently. So that
they can enjoy their state-of-being at genius levels - that is, in tune with
their Doubles. Such a body of people only can really change the
destiny of India.

We have not a trace of doubt about it. Because, the powerful human entity
can be blocked only by disadvantageous settings of mind and intellect.

The Core Recommendations

For Business Organizations and Groups

The implications for human resources development are clear.
Mind-set Analysis needs to be a core: starting with selection, training-development, the design-structuring of teams, and so on IF achieving the genius or entelechy of the organization, institution, etc is of any significance to their owners and top leadership.

The existent managers at all levels are to be sensitized about the mental traps in their mindbergs that block or rebuke their entelechies to become 'creative managers' and 'genius-leaders' - if they 'want' to. For, only a trap-free mind and intellect can be creative and original. Only a creative or original individual can ever be a creative manager or genius-leader. However, such initiatives require the inspiration, support, and involvement of the top-management.

For the Governance Institutions

Sensitize the administrators and officers and executives about their mental traps. This will help them introspect. Encourage them to conduct occasional talks or discussions on mental traps with their colleagues in their work group or total team. The populations of the governance institutions need to open the gates of their minds and intellects - which are closed only by the mental traps. Then, there will be the firm-clear perception that they are there 'by' the people, and actually there 'for' the people.

There is a collective perception that things have gone bad, incorrect, wrong. Therefore, there is the clear requirement of a realisation in the collective consciousness of the reported sample kind of administrators, leaders, and managers that, the life of the entire population of India depends upon their responses, actions, behaviours, and their work.

For B-Schools and other higher-learning centres

Sensitize the 'prospective managers and leaders' about the phenomena of mental traps, the way and pattern in which the traps block even the sensing of the potentialities in them, in the others around, and in the very organization they might join. Sitting in the comfortable class rooms, their 'centricity-conformity trap' misguide them to think that they have become competent in the 'doing' of managing. They are to be sensitized that the carry mental traps along with their bright academic records that really block their creativity, originality, and genius.

The future managers-leaders are to be trained for the level of 'doing' requiredin the VUCA-ness of the imminent times; and for evolving their 'states-of-being'. They are to be exposed to mind-set analysis to get out of various 'boxes' to access their possible-probable originality and creativity. Train them in creative analytic-intellect. So that they resolve and transcend their mental traps, develop creative sensitivity and flexibility, and try original variations in their responses, behaviours, dialogues, actions, and work. B-Schools shall not be a hackneyed version of the primary schools where rote-learning is the salient method.

What is the logic of this recommendation?
Tables 1, 2, and 4 show the state of mental traps of managers as well as B-School entry level students. Out of the senior manager-sample of 1,625 respondents, 735 had done management programs including from the top rated B-Schools. They were not any different fro the non-MBAs. Not any significant difference in analytic thinking, for example.

With medium-to-high-severe mental traps lurking in the no-conscious mindberg the extent to which the management education can induce the required engines to translate the 'knowing' into 'doing' is clearly dubious. Managing is about 'doing' only, which requires engines of the 'being' and freedom from mind-intellect traps. It is the 'being' that does the 'doing'. The traps do not interfere with any 'knowing'. But they definitely negatively intervene the elegance and completeness of 'doing' and 'being'.

For the Nation

A single simple step. Potentially a giant leap towards a 'good-to-great' India. It is to 'sensitize at least a critical mass of the populations of parents, students, and teachers about the mental traps' **Because, no learning, no 'knowing', no 'doing', no 'state-of-being' will ever achieve completeness with mental traps lurking in the mindberg.** Therefore, Mind-set Analysis Workshops must be a critical part in the curriculum. The teachers are to be trained in mind-set analysis and guidance for mental trap resolution. This needs to be done for teachers at the +2 and UG-PG levels in colleges and higher learning centres.

The parents need to take clear responsibility to train the body, mind, and intellect of children to face and manage the ongoing-ensuing VUCA [volatile, uncertain, complex, ambiguous] world and various patterns of crisis in survival-sustenance, work, and relationships.

The children must be provided with or given exposure to as many different, unique, ambiguous, uncertain, new, and strange 'dots' as possible. No doubt, his or her Double will get every one of those 'dots' connected into marvellous design-settings of mind, intellect, spirit; self, work, and leadership qualities.

+++

The core logic of the recommendations
In fact, this book is all bout the logics of these recommendations.

Those who scored 'threshold mental blocks' [optimum required] reported unique, inspiring, and special extra-work-curricular activities and interests, and most of them were recognized at their workplace for their specialities. They appeared a happier and confident lot. Not a single exception among the 87 respondents who scored threshold level mind-sets.

During the workshop processes and class-room sessions significant number of participants improved their self-perception and sense of identity as a potentially creative and original entity. They reported better tuning with work, colleagues, spouses, and children. Their sense of happiness in life increased regardless of the continuity of situations and environment. They happily took the 'Oath of Genius' as genius became their choice and purpose in life, post-workshop. This feedback is significant as it was sought after 8-9 months of training workshops.

Long-term feed-back reported amazing aspects of program-triggered or subsequently-self-discovered shifts in responses, behaviours, actions, dialogues, work, and relationships. They could drop the 'mental traps' on the way. And, they could eventually sense the scope of the original invariant aspect that hides inside and outside. Therefore, the evidence: that, sensitivity to mental traps one's own + also sensing them in others must inevitably trigger a path of 'self-discovery' of the creative dimension of the trinity of mind-intellect-spirit. As well as the 'nirmoksha' of the 'swa-bhavas'.

AND. Almost everyone of those who participated in the workshops and training programs did develop control over their mental traps and sustained their orbits of 'threshold mental blocks' [optimum required]. They could report a shift in perspective. Their expressions, responses, behaviours, actions, work, relationships, and especially language got evolved. Months or years or decades later, they reported unique, inspiring, and special extra-work-curricular activities and interests, and most of them achieved recognition at workplace for their specialities. They could discern their genius in being firm, correct, elegant, taoic, and complete. They claimed living their happiness purpose.

Of course, genius requires a choice, decision, and action. Individuals in the role-functions that provide them the power and authority are in a way, liable to do so. Especially, in this country.

SQAs [Significant Questions and Answers]

A random choice of significant questions and doubts that emerged and were discussed during several training workshops.

Notes:
- Given in the text are more-or-less verbatim transcripts of discussions, question-answer sessions etc from training workshops.
- Seemingly separate concepts-ideas are given under different serial numbers. Whenever the 'questions' or topic was clear in the recording, they are placed as sub-heads.
- You may add your questions and explain your responses. If required, clarification for your questions and responses may be sought through email from: geniusachoice@gmail.com

1
Why should one know about the mental traps?

Yes, good question or doubt. Knowing about mental traps is like getting a feedback about the core state-of-being of your mind. They govern the life, work, relationships, etc of individuals. **Especially, the aspect of 'relationships' - the most complex phenomena in India.**

This knowing about mental traps is a 'feedback'. A feedback that you cannot get from any other sources. A feedback to change your scale of observation of you. See, all learning occurs by 'feedback' signals or messages or parameters available about a performance. When the child makes some 'drawing' the other person gives the feedback, 'A' [in case of writing the capital of English letter]. When you learn the bicycle, your own body gives the feedback that you have got the balance on it. Looking at the feedback from the mirror you verify your face or hairdo.

So, 'feedback' is inevitable for any learning process. Of any process of 'knowing', or 'doing', or about any 'state-of-being'.

Again at advance levels of any doing, you may need the feedback from a mentor or a teacher or a Guru. That is why the ancient Indian idea that 'Guru-sakshaal para-brahma', that is, the Guru is even beyond the 'Brahma', because it is only the Guru who has guided you and provided the feedback: 'Yeah, that's it'.

SO, the very feedback about the type, nature, and extent of mental traps itself is a significant knowing – an awareness about the ways of your non-conscious mindberg. That triggers the very beginning of resolution or vanishing of the traps to a great extent – of course, provided that you have the desire or want to become a 'cat' or 'rose' of your entity. Then, you can devise your own strategies to escape those traps.

You can perhaps, achieve your completeness, 'poornam'. The great Rigvedic verse declares: 'Poornat poornam udacyate': from completeness arises completeness. From incompleteness how can completeness ever originate? Completeness of 'doing' by the completeness of 'being'. The mental traps block the completeness of 'being'. And, all knowing and doing is done by the being.

Werner Heisenberg, the great Physicist, Nobel Laureate too, stated: 'The scale of observation creates the phenomenon'. Reflect upon that fine truth. Then determine that, the knowledge about your mental traps creates a different 'scale' to observe the phenomenon, the very 'you'. You can design a different vantage point to look at your original possible-probable nature. The god-created [or whatever- created] you. The only one of its unique great design-setting-process-product in the history of the species.

2
What is 'Primacy' of MIND?

Key-concept: Primacy
In Psychology, the concept of primacy refers to 'the fact of an item having been presented first to the subject, especially, as it increases its likelihood of being retained and remembered.

The word primacy denotes the fact of being primary, preeminent, or more important [from Latin 'primas': 'of the first rank']

Mind is the first and foremost engine of the human entity. And, mind is the ONLY engine that starts spontaneously and develops almost automatically into its full functional capacity by interaction with the 'significant others' [parents] and by natural variations in the surroundings. Mind carries the supreme power. Beyond body, intelligence, intellect, and perhaps even spirit. Because, it is the first formed engine of the human entity, and it is triggered first, and started functioning first. By its original design-setting-process, the mind is liable to sense the displeasure and discomfort of its carrier: the body and its states and variations. If the mind is not automatically triggered [by the first cry at birth] the entity would die within few hours. Such a design, setting, and process are critical for 'organic survival'. The easiest way to identify the 'primacy of mind' is in the expressions of the infants. The mind initially directs expressions of basic drives of hunger, comfort, safety-security, etc along with corresponding 'emotions'. Later, the need for love and belonging-ness, need for esteem, the need for achievement and power, and finally the need for self-actualization and enlightenment.

The greatness - as well as the cause of the reverse of it - of human beings is in the primacy of the mind. In a way, a human being is nothing but the mind. Her or his entire responses, behaviours, and actions are finally decided or ratified by the mind. The 'inherent analytic-power' of mind is revealed in the emotions, especially of anger and hatred that are directed to others, or anxieties and tensions and fears that are about oneself. At the same time, it has the capacity to hold any emotions without a trace of manifestation. The ultimate or 'peak experience' of enlightenment is vested in the mind. The mind enjoys music and dance, fairy tales and theatre, wisdom and dreaming.

If there was no mind, human beings would not have been able to sense ethics, values, and morals. And if there was no mind, there would not have been the need of them either. There is no issue of ethics among the countless entities of 'sub-human creatures'.

Because, either they have no minds or if at all, they are of a rudimentary level, a minimum threshold function precisely for their level of requirements. Absolutely chaotic doubts or confusions about 'life after death', or about the very death itself is a powerful threat inducing fear-tension-anxiety direct, indirect, subtle, and deep.

In the final analysis, it is true that the greatest of mastery is 'mastery over the mind'. Therefore, develop clarity about the mind. Do not mistake the lack of sensitivity and rigidity as mastery over mind. Instead, know and accept the entire reality of mind vis-a-vis existence flow and then go to the origin or the hub of that wheel of knowing and stay there. If the will, then try to locate the way to the hub of the wheel. Seeing oneself as a wheel. Then locate the hub and its void.

Be firmly clear and do your projective understanding about the following:

- The 'mind' with carries engine powers. It is the first.
- The major part of the mindberg is 'unconscious'.
- That there are the three spokes of non-conscious or unconscious, conscious, and super-conscious to the wheel of your entity.
- That unconscious part stores all the fundamental impressions of early development + moment-to-moment cognitions, perceptions insights, projections, experiences, etc.
- All of human development is by 'learning' unlike birds and cats. Therefore, the forming of mental traps is INEVITABLE in that process of learning and development. Therefore, almost every knowing, doing, and being is susceptible to be driven or governed or intervened by 'mental traps'. Perhaps, the mental traps were essential during childhood.
  But never later.

Therefore, it is inevitable for evolution to resolve the mental traps, IF, an individual wants to become great or to access the powers [creative, original, genius] originally contained in the design-setting-process of a human entity 'owned' and fed; SO, to be managed and led by you.

3
HOW or WHY mental trap sensitivity becomes an advantage?

Reflect upon the following ideas.
Then the advantage of mental- trap sensitivity will be clear.
Knowledge about mental traps must facilitate:

- entry in to the unknown, uncertain, strange, new, unexpected, dangerous, unpredictable future, etc] ...
- interaction with any one with an open and free-wheeling mind and free-floating intellect ...
- easy and comfortable with challenges and potential failures and losses; with the threatening future; with disturbing, demeaning, and defeating relationships, etc ...
- resolution of feelings of humiliation, 'low-ness', and inferiority-feelings
- to proceed in a work or activity despite defeats and self-doubts and resource-myopia ...
- flexibility and variations in expressions, responses, behaviours, dialogues, actions, and relationships; to make creative choices, decisions, and actions ...
- unique and unusual sensitivities and eccentricities ...
- bold choices, decisions, and actions to learn from ways of creativity, originality, and genius ...

As a general technique:
Change your questions to resolve or transcend the mental traps. Even to access enlightenment or Satori. But discover or develop real daring questions. Socratic Questions searching 'evidences'. within you, in your own expressions. Learn to devise Socratic questions. For that, focus attention-to-details of your referent realities. Perhaps, the question needs to be linkageable to the non-conscious of the mindberg. The supreme discoveries are from within. Verified subsequently. Poetry and painting, music and dance, film and theatre are originated inside out of Socratic questions. More or less the same way the 'vagabond' Socrates discovered explanations to every thing he wanted to know and defeated every other mystic of Athens and acclaimed as a great Philosopher [469-399 BC].

4
How the traces of eccentricity can be recreated?
[This book itself is set wit an element of eccentricity].
The very design-setting of human entity is for eccentricity, by eccentricity, and of eccentricity. Universe is eccentric, the design of orbits of planets in the solar system eccentric. The 'tolerance levels' provided for the glandular-physiological functions are for eccentricity required for the managing the random and unpredictable survival climates.

Consider the following evidences:
- Even machines must provide tolerance for eccentricity.
- Every child is eccentric. You, indeed, were a child once upon a time. Every child carries eccentricity. In expressions, responses, behaviours, dialogues, actions, and relationships. Just remember that and reclaim or redeem some of those eccentricities.
- Do a bit of dancing, singing, playing musical instruments, and making little-little devices and toys with your own hands, run around in jungles and forests; take yourself to the world of fairy tales and elegant romantic stories, then to classics and great philosophies.
- Understand eccentricity. Closely observe the invariant tendencies of the varied actions, responses, behaviours of a child between the ages one to nine. Then you will easily get ideas. But beware of mental 'trap-4' [which also implies inspiration suppression, fear of criticism, lowness, humiliation, comments, and comparisons, etc] of the others around. They would feel embarrassed to see you.
- Always remember that you are a victim of not only your mental traps but of others' mental traps too. Perhaps, that is the primary scaffolding for your mental traps.
- Every individual applies the mental 'blocks' to suit their life, work, relationships as well as responses-behaviors-actions-dialogues. Yet, everyone must undergo absolute eccentricities going on live 'inside the mind or consciousness'.
  Evidence: the so-called 'stream of consciousness', the internal monologues, dialogues, and discussions.

Possible-probable that almost unbelievable and even unimaginable kind of thoughts and images and ideas can occur in that stream. Further, 'dreams' are the clear evidences of the original eccentricity of the engines of the intellect: reflection, projection, attention, etc].

- Please be aware that even the so-called worries and anxieties and obsessions, compulsions are primarily eccentric flow. They occur without your agreement. Therefore, fight eccentricity with eccentricity itself. A sword is required to deal with another sword. If you have control or access to your eccentricity, then you can escape the traps of worry, depression, anxiety, etc. That is the beauty of tuning with one's eccentricity: controlled eccentricity. Be aware that no creativity and discovery, innovation - in managerial-leadership work included is possible without the threshold support of eccentricity [of course too much of anything is dangerous and trapping].That is why the mystics, philosophers, geniuses, etc are so cool and detached despite their ultimate sensitivity quotient. They are ultimate eccentrics.
Analytically read their histories for evidences.

- Above all, or at the end of it all, try to see the core invariant of your reality. It is just a 3-dimensional reverse-flow of sensing the signals from the body, mind, and spirit. Just a feedback continuity. Apply or discover ways for a split-second break to that continuity. The axe will hit the head of Satori.

5
WHY Mental Traps remain un-noticed?
Because of the following familiar realms existence:
1. The mental traps are linkaged to motives such as:
   - Safety-security in life, work, and relationships
   - Sexuality
   - Love and Belongingness
   - Self-esteem [fear-tension-anxiety of 'low-ness', inferiority-feeling, humiliation, criticism, etc]
   - self-actualization ideologies commonly known or practised

2. Mental traps are linkaged to Ego Defense Mechanisms [Sigmund Freud] which are also located in the non-conscious of the mindberg.
3. Mental traps are linkaged to the Ego-Advancement Mechanisms of:

> Aggression
> Violent Language
> Hostility
> Jealousy
> Hatred
> Envy
> Manipulation
> Greed for power
> Greed for wealth
> Greed for control

6
The 'super human beings' from the vantage-point of mental traps:
The reported or recorded details of some of the most venerated human beings especially, Jesus, Buddha, and Krishna reveal clear evidences of their trap-free mind, intellect, and tuning with spirit and the resultant will-to-act. You may re-look at their nature and analyse their history of expressions, responses, behaviours, dialogues, actions, work, and relationships from the vantage-point of the 9 mental traps.

The life processes and existential activities are actually based on certain fundamental premises. The non-material nature of assumptions is inter-linked with mental- blocks or mental traps – which again are based on premises and assumptions. So, as everything about existence is assumptions, changing the assumptions behind mental traps can do a lot of miraculous and beautiful or creative and original shifts in the 'self' and its 'state-of-being'.

Therefore, IF you want to change your life, transcend your mental- traps. To repeat, be aware, you ARE nothing but the mind. And mind-settings [total mind] are created by the time-space-location of learning-development, and sustained by choosing to live by those mind-setting.

And mental-blocks or mental traps play the most critical role in the processes of the mind as well as intellect – leading it to its greatness, goodness, or in being good and ethical or driving bad and evil.

+++

The Robert W Weisberg statement may be revised:

"The only difference between the great and the non-great individuals is that, the great individuals were free from mental traps."

7

Political Leaders and Mental Traps

The so-called politicians are likely to have mental traps of medium-to-high orbits. Their 'pattern' of traps is revealed especially in their speeches and actions.

Now that you have understood the nature and dynamics of mental traps you can direct your observation, attention, and conceptualization to differentiate their mental traps. Some of them desire to take control, crave for extra powers or authority more than genuine leadership of populations because of the mental traps of centricity and fear of humiliation and lowness. They are likely to be victims of the fear-tension-anxiety of failure, rigidities, and sensitivity-lag.

However, one thing is clear. The politicians invoke and reinforce the mental traps of populations by cleverly linkaging the fear-tension-anxiety of uncertainty, by invoking centricity and conformity to ideologies, and triggering mental traps related to survival and sustenance and basic motives of the voting populations. The ones who touch the mental-traps most would be the 'voted' leaders. That is the creativity of political leadership..! Perhaps, it is intentionally done as a 'political managing' of the mind-sets of fears and anxieties of the voting populations. Perhaps, there is no other way when the great mass of populations are blocked in their mental traps.

8
Mental Traps and Creative Language Control

Creative Language Control is advantageous in resolving-transcending the mental traps. The advantages of Creative Language Control are as follows:

[1] Creative dialoguing - the core spoke of a creative manager - the significant difference between the usual managers and creative managers. [Creative dialoguing: firmness, elegance, and completeness of 'words-sentences' or concepts and ideas in dialoguing or writing].

[2] For better or creative comprehension of others' languages [words and sentences heard, read, and thought].

[3] For creative conceptualization and re-conceptualization of one's own thoughts, perceptions, mental impressions, experiences, feelings, etc.

[4] Creative 'internal-dialoguing' to evolve and sustain the 'creative self' as well as to 'manage the mind' in the ever 'VUCA' world and operating environment.

[5] Creative attention-to-details for better firmness-clarity of decision making, planning, feedback, guidance, appraisal, etc [language also drives the engine of attention: to translate ideas about mental trap resolution into expressions, responses, behaviours, actions, work, relationships and dialogues]. It requires 'creative-language-control' to write about or to talk about the subtle, invisible, intangible concepts and perspectives, etc;

[6] To deliver 'quality' in language usage, to give an inspiring speech, or to teach, train, guide, mentor higher order 'knowing' or guidelines about 'doing' and to give clues about states-of-being etc requires creative-language-control.

All literature, poetry, philosophical theses, fiction, theoretical perspectives, etc are higher order examples of Creative Language-Control [CLC]. Those creative individuals applied their attention on the way they 'conceptualized' and talked, wrote, and lived.

Education rulers-leaders [policy makers and administrators], clerics [curriculum, textbook, syllabus, pedagogy etc designers], and traders [schools, universities, professional institutes, etc] need to develop sensitivity about the evidences that indicate defeating orbits of reality for the so-called beneficiaries - young pristine minds. They must design the setting and process of education to provide clear 'evidences' to the learning-and-development of children. Instead of the centricity and conformity maintained paper Degrees alone. The decades of rote-learning does convert them more and more into 'trap-infected' minds-intellects-spirits.

The management students should be given assignment of writing book-reviews on one of three books: Organization Entelechy: Creative Manager, Genius Leader, Taoic Process; or The Missing Engines of Management Education, or the Master Thief: Stealing sources inside. Every manager shall read and reflect upon the ideas in those books. Then they will know what to do by and in their 'doing' and how to manage their 'being'.

9
Mental traps and self-discovery or Satori
Absence of mental traps [or 'threshold mental-blocks'] cannot automatically invoke tuning with the attendant spirit or Satori. Yet such a state-of-being guarantees the scope for self-discovery. An invariable prerequisite for Satori. Good engine-powered vehicle owned by a person does not automatically entail his or her competency despite great desire to drive it.

The great Krishna had to 'talk' [conveying ideas and concepts and perspectives] for days to Arjuna to convince him to take arms against the oppressive opponents. Actually, you must read only self realisation etc books. For that is your ultimate drive in life. No substitute. Fame and awards and money etc no replacement at all. Enlightenment is like getting the dots connected in correct linkages - in retrospect. No planned systematically induced dots. For the genius music director, there are virtually no boundaries. But for any of his songs, there will be clear boundaries and restrictions. The singers get trapped in the boundaries.

Anyway, there will be several dots getting spontaneously connected back by the end of the journey. The dots may have occurred coincidently or by tuning with the path of life, or planned interventions to achieve and to ensure success, power and control; dots of good-right-correct or dots of incorrect-wrong-bad. If there are a lot of bad and wrong dots, it will be tragedy. So choose and decide on good and wonderful and beautiful dots.

We are setting up the Geniuschoice Institute and the Genius Temple for training in self realisation or Satori also. By training in freewheeling mind, the engines of intellect for referent-reality perception, and creative language control.

The difference between self-real-isation and self actual-ization
Self realisation is one step above self actualization. Both are different. Or opposite even. A good number of people may achieve self actualization of their goals, plans, dreams, wishes, purposes etc that defined the salient drives of their 'self'. Money, fame, riches, 'good' jobs and homes, marriage of children, writing book create dance, music, films, etc create and provide leadership to an organization or ideology, institution, etc. But realisation of self is different. It is in discerning the nature of the very so-called self [that aspires to actualise or realise included]. The 'knowing' and 'doing' are different for reali-isation and actual-ization. The resultant state-of-being is greatly different. One is no mind. Other, a mind molested by traps of fears and anxieties.

Mastering the engine of attention to drive into details
There is no great scope for attention to details in reading a book or in language per se. Because in language the words and sentences mean a definite thing and you understand that. Attention to details is relevant only when you come across the referent reality of words-sentences. You can pay attention to the details of the matchbox but to what details you will attend to in the 'word' M-A-T-C-H-B-O-X. Nothing.

The word Matchbox just names a thing, matchbox. But, when you get a real matchbox before you, or in your hand, there is great range of details about it. Got the point?

You have to become an embodiment of attention. You have to become 'an attention having a body'. Then only you can really feel so called enlightened or satori state which is all the time with you. When it is pointed out in a very close interaction and very correct language someone may get a glimpse of that. But still it will not be captured because the attention is looking at it from a distant orbit. So you have to become attention itself. A cat is attention. A bird is attention itself. All creatures are like that. That is why they are able to locate things and survive. A cat is in full attention when it looks at that point and exactly jumps and lands on the brim of a wall without a single trial.

Swami Vivekananda was talking about that attention ['concentration' in the quote, page 196]. By practice you get that attention on the bicycle so that you can balance it on rope 80 feet tall. Or you play Tabla, Sitar or Tabla, or guitar without even looking at it. Your body becomes guitar itself. So that is what I call attention. You just pay attention to the music and your body plays it. That level of attention is required when you want to play the guitar of enlightenment too. Let the rulers, clerics, and traders reflect upon the nature and dynamics of their 'attention'. Let all types of leaders and managers, administrators, and students, reflect or a minute about the completeness and elegance of their 'doings' and 'being'.

Special Note on the 'Double'

The concept of Double refers to that which drives, executes, and coordinates all the 'doings' of the human entity or any entity. All the learned 'doings' are 'duplicates' of those that exist as doings and things in the environment. There is the Double also of the being of a human entity That is the ultimate.

The 'doing' or actual execution of neuro-muscular movements in coordinated way to perform a certain action or set of actions – is driven by the Double. Every learning is finally with the Double. The learning can be such as eating or talking or singing, thinking meditating or cycling or writing and so on.

The possible-probable whatever kind of 'doing' - including the 'doing' of 'knowing' or reading and learning something, as well as gross actions of walking eating, running, etc are executed by the Double. For example: it is the Double that 'learns' a song after repeated listening to it.

The evidence of 'balance-upon-bicycle' can be considered for discerning the nature of the possible reality of the Double. See, once you have learned and mastered the bicycle – actually you gained sort of a ' duplicate copy' of the bicycle. See, if the bicycle did something on its own intentionality, it would have done pedaling itself moving forward in balance. But, it is a mechanical device, so no life its own. By practicing for few days, you get the duplicate of it's 'balance'. A circus girl is in tune with that Double completely.

Now you got the balance of the bicycle, but what you have done? No clarity. But, you just behaved wit it for some time despite fall and injuries. One day you discover the balance of it - inside you. But what happened is that, you got a 'duplicate', <u>a duplicated impression of the way of the balance of the bicycle</u> - if the cycle had done that balancing on its own. You got a duplicate of the bicycle inside you. It is the case with your 'balance' in language. By constant interface with the languages of others around, you got the Double of it. You can get the Double of virtually any activity, entity, thing, process, phenomena in the world. Not only the world out side. But of the world inside - such as the Double of that cycle of respiration. Or even the Double of the very human entity with you.

Double is not at all the so-called 'atman or psyche or self or spirit'. They are all, perhaps, aspects of the 'being'. It took a lot of 'behaving with it' to get the 'balance' – to do walking, writing, eating, dancing, talking, singing, etc. The balance on the intellect engines of attention, thinking, reflection, dreaming, etc may take much more extent and height of 'behaving'. With sword-sharp and sword-speed attention to details of what is going on when you do something, such as cooking a tea, or giving music to a lyric, you will directly even 'sense' whatever is named Double. You will know that everything is just duplicated in your entity, or in its consciousness or Central-Nervous-System electrical fields, or whatever.

Now, when you really 'behave' or interact with the bicycle that is you, when you are aware that you are on that supreme bicycle of you, then you will get the balance on the Double of your human entity.

The Double of the human entity: The source of 'Originality'
Once you develop sensitivity to the Double of the entity, you, albeit non-consciously, then onwards your 'being' will be 'original'. You will respond-act-talk with 'originality' You do not have to 'plan' or 'think' in advance for a complex 'doing', or prepare for any action, or speech, or meeting, etc. Nor panicky about loss of money, or reaching a place on time, getting a thing done on time, etc. Your 'being' will execute the required actions correct, elegant, and complete.

As an example of the way Double-of-the Entity functions by 'originality' or 'out of no preparation' in the case of creating music is perhaps, the case of the genius music director Illayaraja. He creates music taking virtually no time. He composed 6 songs each for 6 films [36 songs] in just one hour. In a TV interview* Illayaraja declares as follows [half translation]:

> "I don't think' in order to compose music... i don't need to 'think' to create music... 'thinking is the problem'... if you think, 'only the mental condition will reflect in the tune'... 'thinking is not required'... once the situation is explained, whatever tune comes, IS the tune... **It has to come on its own**... we cannot create it... if we create it, our 'mental condition' will reflect in it... [repeated] 'that is what is happening everywhere'...'**I myself don't know how it is coming, it is very difficult thing to explain how it is coming**'... all other music directors have had their training, but I have had no training... 'how much of music I know' is not important, 'but **music knows about me', that is why it happens...**"

Such an 'originality' is possible by the Double in any chosen domain of 'doing'. If one has the 'being' of free-wheeling mind and intellect.

*Illayaraja interviewed by Johny Lukose, Manorama News Channel:
 'Interview with Illayaraja - Rajapattu | Manorma News'

The PNK-Questionnaire

Read each statement given, and write in, in the brackets [ ] the appropriate letter [1, 2, 3, or 4 as shown in the response categories] to indicate your opinion on each statement. Since it is a standardized instrument, indicate your responses correctly. Do not leave any items.

RESPONSE CATEGORIES

1 : Strongly Disagree   2 : Disagree
3 : Agree   4 : Strongly Agree

1. [ ] I prefer a boss who tells precisely what I am supposed to do
2. [ ] Women should not dress like men and vice versa
3. [ ] You can make out what people are likely noticing the way they dress
4. [ ] I don't like to compete with strong opponents
5. [ ] You can't be called mature unless you can really control your emotions
6. [ ] At work or studies I generally don't share problems with friends or colleagues and seek their guidance
7. [ ] I really dislike any criticism levelled against me
8. [ ] I resist expressing tenderness towards others
9. [ ] I hate confusion
10. [ ] One must fulfill one's social obligations at any cost
11. [ ] Necessities must always have priority over artistic matters
12. [ ] I hate to lose at games
13. [ ] I rather dislike sad movies
14. [ ] I don't think I can do well in a job or activity different from my field of experience or learning
15. [ ] I like to make friends mostly with those who appreciate me
16. [ ] I have very little interest in flower arrangements and things like that
17. [ ] If you don't plan your holidays in detail, you just end up wasting time and money
18. [ ] Premarital sex is wrong because it is considered immoral

19. [ ] People in the same profession have similar personalities
20. [ ] In a meeting I don't speak up unless I am an expert on a point
21. [ ] No matter what choice of food I have in a restaurant prefer
       to order my favourites
22. [ ] One can accomplish little without the support of the authorities
23. [ ] I feel tense communicating with person who have greater
       authority than I
24. [ ] Enjoying the pleasures of the body or high material comforts
       detracts from high thinking
25. [ ] I dislike unfamiliar situations
26. [ ] There is a great danger in giving up our old customs
27. [ ] I can predict the behavior of a person if I know his or her
       social background
28. [ ] I dislike being compared to others
29. [ ] I have never bothered myself with modern art and the like
30. [ ] I don't think I have any very distinctive skills outside my area
       of specialization
31. [ ] I don't like being contradicted in the presence of others
32. [ ] I cannot be bothered with questions such as 'what would happen if
       birds had brain like humans and humans had wings like birds' and so on
33. [ ] I cannot stand meetings without a clear prior agenda
34. [ ] Parents know best what occupations their children should pursue
35. [ ] I am more comfortable after I have classified a person
36. [ ] I prefer to give up when I hear that a task is too difficult
37. [ ] A pound of imagination is not worth an ounce of facts
38. [ ] I don't think India has the resources to catch up with the West
39. [ ] I dislike juniors trying to be familiar or friendly with me
40. [ ] I don't like to go to serious movies

NOTE:
Feedback is advantageous whether positive or negative. If you want to know the extent of your mind-sets, as to 'blocks' or 'traps', fill in and send the responses vis-a-vis item numbers [1 to 40] to email: geniusachoice@gmail.com

THE SAMPLE DETAILS

Government-Administration Officers

1. Institute of Management in Government, Kakkanad, Kerala [278]
2. Kerala Government [98]
3. Bihar government [185]
4. LBSNAA [48] – Probationers of IFS, IAS, and IPS cadres
5. LBSNAA [25] – Joint Secretary level Officers
    Sub-total: 634

+++

B-School Students

1. Chandragupt Institute of Management Patna [587] – nine batches of management students
2. IIM-Kozhikode [132]
3. Trivandrum Engineering College [60] Management students
4. Rajagiri Institute of Social Sciences [90] – two batches of PM&IR Students
5. Rajagiri College of Business Studies, Kakkanad [180] – 3 batches of Management students
6. TKM Institute of Management, Kollam [180] – 4 batches of management students
7. Amrita Institute of Management, Edappaly [50]
8. TA Pai Institue of Management [TAPMI], Manipal [60] Management students
9. GRD Institute of Management, Coimbatore [35] Management students
10. PSG Institute of Management, Coimbatore [180] Management students
    TOTAL B-Schools students: 1,554
    Males: 773   Females: 781

+++

PUBLIC SECTOR Organizations

Managers [various levels, including VPs, GMs, and CEOs]

1. Kerala State Nirmiti Kendra, Trivandrum [45] - Architects
2. Kochi refineries [128] – over a duration of 7 years, various levels of managers, engineers, fresh recruits, etc
3. Indian Additives Ltd, Chennai [29] - Engineers, Managers
4. Hindustan Latex Ltd, Trivandrum [25] - Managers
5. Hindustan Latex Ltd, Belgaum [30] - Managers
6. MILMA, Trivandrum [62] – Senior Managers
7. Kerala Feeds Ltd [28] - Managers
8. Kerala State Cooperative Bank Ltd, Trivandrum [45] - Branch Heads
9. Kerala State Electricity Board, Trivandrum [26] - Senior Engineers
10. MATSYAFED, Govt. of Kerala, Trivandrum [52] - Managers
11. Coir Corporation, Kerala State [50] - Managers
12. Cochin Port Trust [23] - Senior Officers
13. Hindustan Organics Ltd, Ambalamugal [45] - Managers
14. Indian Navy [84] - Senior Officers
15. NTPC, Kayamkulam [32] - Engineers
    SUB TOTAL: 704

+++

PRIVATE SECTOR MANAGERS [VARIOUS LEVELS]

1. Thermax Limited, Pune [48] - Senior Managers
2. TVS Lucas [18] – 1st ring of Senior Managers, Division Heads
3. Mafatlal Industries Ltd, Mumbai [105] - Managers
4. Indian Express Bombay Ltd [125] - Manager levels
5. IIM-Kozhikode, [124] - MDP participants
6. Eicher Volvo Motors Ltd, Indore [82] - Engineers
7. Kottakkal Aryavydya Pharmacy [18] - Top Management team
8. Muthoot Ceramics, Kochi [30] - Managers
9. Masoneilan India Ltd, Kochi [30] - Engineers
10. Crompton Greaves Ltd, Global R&D Division, Mumbai [82] - Research Scientists

11. Crompton Greaves Ltd, Mumbai [25] - Marketing Managers
12. Apollo Tyres Ltd, Perambra, Kerala [64] – managers
13. Indian Aluminium Company Limited, Kalamassery [120] - Junior, Middle, and Top Management including Unit CEOs
14. AVT McCormick Ltd, Alwaye [45] - Senior Managers
15. Group of companies [MDP] [35] - Top and Senior Managers
    Private sector managers N: 951

+++

Large IT organizations

1. Infosys, Bangalore + Pune [265]
2. Satyam Computers Ltd, Chennai [275]
3. RAMCO Systems, Chennai [35]
4. Hexaware Technologies Ltd., Chennai, Mumbai, Bangalore, Pune [202]

Medium-Small IT Organizations
[Project Leaders and Owners]

5. Guildsoft Private Limited. Trivandrum [34]
6. GIWIA [IT company], Alwaye, Kerala [25]
7. Ivorysoft [IT company], Ernakulam, Kerala [30]
8. Ceredian Infotech Ltd [38]
9. AT&T, Pune [23]
10. Thermax Infotech [25]
11. Skycell, Chennai [30]
12. Team Frontline Pvt. Ltd. [42]
13. Ipath India Pvt Ltd [28]
14. Small IT units [13] : 175
    Sub-total: 1207

+++

GRAND TOTAL OF 'CORPORATE' SAMPLE: 5,050

This sample is apart from the larger sample of 13,365 respondents.

214

Gratitude to Shri. Ashok Harris,
COO, Hexaware Tehnologies Ltd.
For his genuine and unconditional support.
Gratitude also to Aparna Jayram and her team of
Madhuparna Nandi, Muruganantham, Serene Banerjee, et al
of Hexavarsity for coordinating several MSAWs for over 3 years.

Gratitude
to Dr. Pradip N Khandawalla,
the creator of the foundation-Questionnaire that steered
this report and the inspiration for searching the dynamics
of mental traps by the creative perceptions
revealed in his wonderful books listed below.
[Doctoral Guide of Prasad Sundararajan].

The books of Pradip N Khandwalla, in Amazon.in

Lifelong Creativity: An Unending Quest [2011]
Corporate Creativity: The Winning Edge [2017]
Creative Society: Prospects for India [2014]
Management of Corporate Greatness: Blending Goodness
    With Greed [2009]
Revitalizing the State: A Menu of Options [1999]
Design of Organizations [1977]
Fourth Eye: Excellence Through Creativity: A Fresh Approach to
    Effective Management of Individual, Organizational, and
    Social Creativity [2000]
Social Development: A New Role for the Organizational Sciences
[1989]
Innovative Corporate Turnarounds [1992]
Fast Forward Towards Civilizational Greatness: Agenda for India
[2018]

And books of his poetry...

This work is dedicated.

- To the leaders and managers of organizations and institutions | management students | governance administrators | leaders of all domains of social significance ... who want to initiate and conduct creative shifts in the destinies their own and of their domains of activities, workplaces, colleagues, and their families, institutions, and organizations.

- To those who want to be inspired to discover the 'originality' in them. To be firm-correct-elegant-tuned and complete in their knowing | doing | being.

- To those who 'want to be great' | to manifest their entelechy or 'Swa-Bhava-Nirmoksha' in the expressions, responses, behaviours, actions, and dialogues | self, work, and relationships.

- To the parents | teachers | guides | mentors | trainers.

- To the entelechy of the genius-loci of India.

THE 9 MENTAL TRAPS OF CORPORATE INDIA

Director of the Work	Dr. Prasad Sundararajan
Producer of the Work	Dr. V Mukunda Das
Inspiration of the story	The Double

CREW

FROM CHANDRAGUPT INSTITUTE OF MANAGEMENT PATNA

Dr. Priyanka Sinha
Dr. Jyoti Verma
Dr. Debabrata Samanta
Prof. GK Murthy
Rajeev Ranjan
Deepak Sharma
Sumit Kumar
Rejith Krishnan

FROM THE GENIUSCHOICE INSTITUTE AND THE GENIUS TEMPLE, KALIMANAGALAM, COIMBATORE

Dr. Tharanath Sankunni
Dr. Priya Meenakshi
Ameya Rajarishi
VinayLal
Veena Ganesh
Arati Bhadra
Divya Bhadrakumar

GRATEFUL CREDITS   5,050 + 13,365 Participants + Respondents

Cover Drawing by Rishiga Tripurasundari
'The butterfly of creativity, originality, and genius of human entities
  is blocked, choked, and crippled by something called mental traps'.

Picture of the 'The Cook Stealing the Art of Sword ' by Urvi Devarshi

Dr. V Mukunda Das

Director,
Chandragupt Institute of Management Patna

Dr. Prasad Sundararajan

Researcher, Genius Temple, Geniuschoice Institute.
Involved in researching mind-intellect-spirit,
creativity, originality, genius, eccentricity, etc since
1974. Authored 6 books: 'See You', 'Genius Choice',
'Organizational Entelechy: Creative Manager,
Genius Leader, Taoic Process', 'Missing Engines of
Management Education', 'The Master Thief: Stealing
Sources Inside', and 'Hail Logos'. Visiting Professor
at Chandragupt Institute of Management Patna.

www.ingramcontent.com/pod-product-compliance
Lightning Source LLC
Chambersburg PA
CBHW051308220526
45468CB00004B/1250